Double Your Success proliferates the intentional desire of two very determined men to plan the work of creating a multimillion-dollar business. They worked their plan and put in the required hands-on hard work—coupled with solid business practices, personal will, and follow-through—to make the book as well as multiple successful businesses a reality. This must-read book is one that you won't want to put down. It is a step-by-step process of applied principles that helped the authors get to a directed goal with replicable results. *I love it!*

Dr. Robert Bostic
superintendent, Stafford Municipal School District

The Carters have basically condensed several business courses into an easy-to-read handbook for success. They literally provide both the practical and the academic pathway to entrepreneurial success. Whether you are considering opening a business, just started one, or are well along your way, this book is a *must*-read.

Dr. Austin Lane
president, Texas Southern University

Inked by two phenomenal brothers, this book brings to life keys to success that will inspire and equip readers to achieve greatness in their business ventures.

Tandra C. Jackson
office managing partner, Houston, KPMG LLP

DOUBLE

your

SUCCESS

DOUBLE *your* SUCCESS

PRINCIPLES TO BUILD A
MULTIMILLION-DOLLAR BUSINESS

STEPHEN LEVI CARTER, MBA

DR. STERLING L. CARTER

ForbesBooks

Published by ForbesBooks, Charleston, South Carolina.
Member of Advantage Media Group.

ForbesBooks is a registered trademark, and the ForbesBooks colophon is a trademark of Forbes Media, LLC.

Printed in the United States of America.

10 9 8 7 6 5 4 3 2 1

ISBN: 978-1-946633-45-3
LCCN: 2018954456

Cover and layout design by George Stevens.

This publication is designed to provide accurate and authoritative information in regard to the subject matter covered. It is sold with the understanding that the publisher is not engaged in rendering legal, accounting, or other professional services. If legal advice or other expert assistance is required, the services of a competent professional person should be sought.

Advantage Media Group is proud to be a part of the Tree Neutral® program. Tree Neutral offsets the number of trees consumed in the production and printing of this book by taking proactive steps such as planting trees in direct proportion to the number of trees used to print books. To learn more about Tree Neutral, please visit **www.treeneutral.com**.

Since 1917, the Forbes mission has remained constant. Global Champions of Entrepreneurial Capitalism. ForbesBooks exists to further that aim by bringing the Stories, Passion, and Knowledge of top thought leaders to the forefront. ForbesBooks brings you The Best in Business. To be considered for publication, please visit **www.forbesbooks.com**.

To our mother, Arnell White. You gave of yourself unselfishly, sacrificing personally, professionally, and financially to raise two little boys whom you loved with all of your heart. All that we are, do, and have is because of you. We love you.

Acknowledgements

For many years, we have talked about writing a book detailing our plight. We realized that writing a book is sort of like building a business. It can take a lot more to start it than just having a dream. Along the way, a number of people helped push us to this goal.

To our aunt and godmother, Edith. You have always been there for us as a mentor, a second mother, a confidant, and a role model. We will always be indebted to you for loving us like your own children.

To our deceased father, Maceo. You made your way to heaven when we were only twelve years old. Although our time together was short, you made an everlasting impact on our lives. We titled our parent company in your name: Maceo Carter Investments, LLC. We will always love you.

To dear Langston. Langston University was the foundation from which all that we have achieved was first birthed. This small, historically black university in the red dirt of Oklahoma taught us that anything is possible. Mother Langston built friendships and networks that will last our lifetime. We will always hold you dear to our hearts. From Langston to the world!

To our esteemed brothers of the Men's Forum: Chris, Macque, and Robert. You have been our inspiration for over twenty-five years. We have pushed each other to greater heights. We have cried together, laughed together, fought together, lost together, and won together. You are our true friends.

To our cousin, Cortez Carter. You have been a role model and a mentor even when you did not know that you were. A true renaissance man who was our example of how anything was possible. Thanks for showing us that anything is possible.

From Sterling:

To my wife, Crystal, and stepson, Garry. Thank you for bringing so much joy and laughter into my life. Thank you for continued support, love, and patience. You both inspire me to do more and to push even harder so that I may provide you with everything you have ever wished for. I have learned how to become selfless and think of family first. I am forever indebted to you both.

From Stephen:

To my wife, Daphane. Thank you for supporting and loving me throughout the years. Through every hair-brained idea I came up with, business I started, venture I took us on, you've always been there. You are my rock. Your intelligence, work ethic, and beautiful personality has given me the fuel to keep pushing even when I thought of giving up. You are my greatest achievement.

To my children, Yasmine, Madison, and Morgan. You all are the wind beneath my wings. The fire to keep me going. I pray that I am an example of what is possible when you stay the course despite the struggles and obstacles. I love you dearly.

TABLE OF CONTENTS

About the Authors

Dr. Sterling L. Carter has been a licensed physical therapist since 1997. He holds bachelor's degrees from Langston University in biology and physical therapy, a master's degree in physical therapy with a focus on orthopedics from Texas Woman's University, and a clinical doctorate in physical therapy from Simmons College in Boston. Sterling is also a certified strength and conditioning specialist.

Sterling has proudly served in active and reserve status in the US Army since 1987, and retired in 2017 at the officer rank of major (promotable). He is a decorated soldier with two commendation medals and two achievement medals, a certified combat medical specialist, and is a graduate of the Officers' Basic and Officers' Advanced schools in addition to the US Army Commander and General Staff College. He is a Saudi Arabia Service Medal recipient, and he served as the executive officer of a US Army hospital unit, overseeing the direction and care of over three hundred and fifty soldiers. After serving as a combat medic in Operation Desert Storm in 1990–1991 with his twin brother, Stephen, while still in his teens, Sterling returned to the

United States and completed his physical therapy degree and began working at a variety of hospitals in the Houston area. Sterling was called to serve once again in 2006–2007; under Operation Iraqi/ Enduring Freedom, he cared for soldiers coming from Iraq and Afghanistan with major injuries and significant trauma. Returning home to the United States after that tour of duty, Sterling opened his own clinic, Sterling Physical Therapy and Wellness, in 2008. From the start, Sterling Physical Therapy and Wellness has had a reputation as a clinic that patients can turn to for quality care with results.

In 2011, Sterling provided the initial vision, network, brand, and extensive health care experience for the launch of Sterling Staffing Solutions where he holds the position of COO and Partner. He has also launched Sterling Physical Therapy & Wellness of Sugar Land (2008), SPTW Transportation Services LLC (2011) and Sterling Physical Therapy & Wellness of Houston (2015).

Stephen Levi Carter, MBA has been a finance and management professional for more than two decades. He earned a bachelor's of business administration in accounting from Langston University. His college years were interrupted by service as a US Army combat medic, alongside his twin brother, Sterling, in Operation Desert Storm. Upon returning home from Iraq, he immediately returned to Langston University to complete the bachelor's degree he'd started before the war. He also holds a master of business administration in change management and finance from the University of Houston Clear Lake. Stephen is also a certified project management professional (PMP), the most important industry-recognized certification for project managers.

Stephen's career in finance has included managerial and executive-level positions for consulting firms, medical insurance companies, oil and gas companies, and technology firms. Stephen has specialized in ERP systems and software package implementations within organizations assisting in managing day-to-day business activities such as accounting, procurement, project management and manufacturing. Additionally, he has been responsible for "turn-around" activities where he has been charged with improving the overall performance of processes, departments, divisions or entire companies.

As an entrepreneur, Stephen has owned multiple businesses, including a digital publishing platform, a public relations and promotions company, a beauty and grooming studio, a upscale restaurant, and a full-service accounting and tax consulting firm.

In 2011, Stephen left the corporate world to provide the initial capital, business intellect, and operational strategy in forming Sterling Staffing Solutions with his brother, Sterling. Today, he serves as CEO and partner of Sterling Staffing Solutions and is CEO of White Orchid Hospice LLC (2017), a hospice company providing palliative and hospice services to patients throughout the greater Houston metropolitan area.

Foreword

From the moment I met Stephen and Sterling in the early nineties, the impression left on me was one of passion and focus on making a mark in the world through achieving their individual and collective goals. Their success is not by mistake or happenstance. I have watched as they have learned from every experience and applied lessons learned to help ensure a better tomorrow for their family, friends, employees, and colleagues. In this book, these brothers are inviting you into their world by sharing their keys to successfully growing your business. Today, as I am honored to pen this foreword, I realize how these brothers continue to have that same passion and focus in their personal and professional endeavors. And like all great leaders, for them it's not enough to simply achieve success, but through sharing these principles, they are seeking to achieve *significance*. This comes from caring, sharing, and shining a light on the path for others to follow. I encourage you to enjoy the ride and be prepared to take advantage of the insights provided by entrepreneurs who wish you nothing but success in all that you do. *Double Your Success* stands as a testament to the Carters' uncompromising passion and focus to share their *successes* and achieve *significance*.

It is not often you find people who willingly share their keys to success. In this book, the Carters provide sound principles that, if followed, will help the readers achieve new heights in their respective businesses. For example, in principle two, the Carters explore the importance of planning and defining the reason why your business idea is one that will be well received in the marketplace. Like with any planning process, you must objectively explore your chosen market, what you have to offer, and then develop a plan to execute your idea and compete. It has been said it takes years to become an overnight success. This could not be more appropriate than in the life of a business owner. Principle four redefines "overnight success" and helps the reader to realize there is no such thing, and that only through a disciplined, well-thought-out approach can entrepreneurs expect to build and grow their businesses. "Good enough" never is. Principle ten encourages the reader to stay hungry and explains very clearly that if you aren't improving, you are losing the race. Never settle for good. Seek to continuously improve, and the insights shared through the principles in the book are of value to new entrepreneurs and seasoned professionals alike.

Starting a business is no easy task, and growing the business is even more daunting at times. Through this journey there will be ups, downs, and times when doubt may creep in. The Carters' well-organized approach detailed in *Double Your Success* will give the reader the advantage of learning from entrepreneurs who have been where they are, and who have grown their business into a multimillion-dollar enterprise from humble beginnings. This book is an absolute must-read for those who seek to start and grow their respective businesses to levels beyond their wildest dreams, and it should serve as encouragement to strive towards *success* while achieving *significance*.

During the past twenty-five plus years, I have watched Stephen and Sterling live what they have written. In this book, you as the reader gain the benefit of these life experiences as they are memorialized for your review, study, and reference. I am incredibly proud of my friends, and I applaud them as they have opened themselves up in this book for all to see and learn from them. I advise you to get out your note pads and highlighters on this journey, and get ready to *Double Your Success.*

Jeffrey Webber
president/CEO
AltairStrickland

Introduction

It's surprising to many people to hear about our upbringing. Why? Because seeing where we are today, it's clear that we've accomplished much in our lives despite our humble beginnings. Today we are owners of a very successful health care staffing agency—a very different place from where we started.

We are twin brothers descended from Mississippi sharecroppers. Our parents learned the value of hard work in the cotton fields and farmlands in the deep South, and they instilled that work ethic in us at an early age. Our parents both came from large families of eight-plus siblings, which also taught them the value of making a dollar stretch and the art of sharing—two disciplines that we have worked to emulate over the years.

As young adults, our parents left the fields for other lines of work. Our father became a noncommissioned officer in the US Air Force, leaving his home in Shubuta, Mississippi, to travel the world on Uncle Sam's dime. Our mother, born in Prentiss, Mississippi, had a long career in education teaching hospitality management and what was then known as home economics. After meeting and marrying, our parents moved to Houston, where we were born, and where our father was assigned to the Ellington Air Force Base.

Although ours was a very loving family, our father struggled with post-traumatic stress disorder as a result of his war tours, including one with the Vietnam conflict. He passed away when we were quite young, and we spent most of our childhood years in a single-parent household. Our mother was an amazing woman who, in addition to teaching, worked multiple jobs to ensure that we never went without what we needed. Other family members, such as Aunt Edith, as well as other various special people, sometimes stepped in to help raise us.

In spite of our circumstances, our mom wanted us to attend college—she viewed education as the great equalizer, and was one of the first in her family to earn a master's degree. Without the funds to put two kids through college at the same time, our mother pointed to the GI Bill with the US military as our opportunity for free schooling. In 1987, our junior year of high school, we signed up with the US Army Reserves on the buddy system. We were seventeen years old.

We both scored very high on the Armed Services Vocational Aptitude Battery competency exam, which qualified us to enter the medical field, and we both elected to become combat medics, or medical specialists.

After graduating high school, we went to Fort Sill, the US Army base in Oklahoma, for boot camp. Once we completed basic training, we were required to serve one weekend per month throughout the year and two full weeks during the summer months. We served at a hospital unit in Oklahoma while attending Langston University, where we both had academic and music scholarships that, combined with the GI Bill, covered most of the cost of our tuition. College was where we learned the importance of multitasking and prioritization. Having to juggle military service, maintaining a B-plus average to keep our academic scholarships, performing in the marching and symphonic bands, being engaged in social and business organizations, and holding part-time jobs and internships during the summers was a challenge.

In 1990, our sophomore year in college, we were called to serve in Operation Desert Storm. We started our service in the Persian Gulf War together but then were separated, with one of us going to serve in a field artillery unit while the other served in a hospital evacuation unit. We served in Saudi Arabia and Iraq, and we were headed to Baghdad when the war concluded.

During our time overseas, we learned a lot at a very young age while taking care of our fellow soldiers and Iraqi soldiers. We actually turned twenty-one while at war in the desert—or "the sandbox," as we called it.

Fortunately, we both returned from the war unharmed, and at the young age of twenty-one, we were US Army war veterans.

After our service, we both finished our undergraduate degrees and pursued careers in different industries—health care and oil and gas, respectively. But over time, as a need for health care staffing became apparent, we combined our experiences and joined together to form our company Sterling Staffing Solutions.

We've had great success in our venture, and we've learned a considerable amount about business, leadership, mentoring, and giving of yourself to others. We wrote this book to share our insights into how to grow a successful business in a short time frame by applying certain principles. We also wrote this book for our family and friends, and for young people who are struggling and need inspiration to pursue a different path in life. We want others to see that hurdles can be overcome—nothing is insurmountable if you are driven to succeed, in either your personal or your professional life.

Nothing is insurmountable if you are driven to succeed, in either your personal or your professional life.

This is designed to be a "handbook" of information. We have developed eleven business principles that, if followed, will help you build a successful multimillion-dollar business. We want you to be able to turn to the principle that contains the information you need and then refer back to it as needed.

The principles ahead are divided into sections:

- Section I is about the planning stages of any venture. This section discusses:

  - defining your niche and determining your "why";

  - the value of researching your idea, along with tips for planning and goal setting;

  - the importance of relationships; and

  - understanding that there is no such thing as an "overnight success."

- Section II is about implementing your venture. This section discusses:

- tips for selling your vision to stakeholders; and

- the CARES model, which stands for compassion, attitude, respect, excellence, and servant leadership.

- Section III is about the leader's mindset. This section discusses:

  - the definition of a servant leader;

  - the value of coaching and mentoring; and

  - taking your venture to the next level.

- Section IV is about identifying and dealing with pitfalls. This section discusses:

  - if you are not improving, you are losing the race; and

  - preparing for disasters.

We hope you will find the principles ahead to be an interesting read and a valuable resource as you pursue your own path to success.

SECTION I

PLANNING

Define Your Niche

Amazing insights can come from adverse situations. That certainly happened to us in the wake of Hurricane Harvey. What would turn out to be a category four hurricane devastated our city, Houston, Texas, in August 2017. The 280-mile-wide storm had winds of 130 miles per hour, and would ultimately dump fifty-one inches of rain on Texas.[1] Some thirty thousand people were left without shelter, and early estimates placed the damage at $75 million in loss of property.[2]

Harvey flooded the streets of Houston in a matter of hours. What started with only a few inches of rain in the street quickly became floodwaters that reached doorsteps. By morning, with rain still falling and wind still churning, there was a foot or two of water inside homes and businesses. Those residents who chose to wait out the storm found themselves without options and needing to be rescued to escape the waters rising inside their homes.

It was an abysmal situation for residents and businesses alike. In one day, our health care staffing company went from conducting business as usual to scrambling to find employees, contractors, and the patients we serve. In preparation ahead of the storm, we had set up a group text message system to ensure that we could communicate with our team, but it never occurred to us that the communication systems themselves, which we relied on so heavily, would let us down. When the storm hit, it took down many cell towers, and with them, the internet that we relied on to stay in touch with staff. While the company still had service, many of the people we were trying to reach did not.

Since we provide staffing personnel for serving patients in their homes, we had multiple levels of concern. We had to communicate with our office staff to keep operations running, we had to locate the therapists who provided patient care, we had to communicate with the home health companies that we contracted with, and we had to find the patients who were in need of care—some of which was critical for the patient's survival. But with so many people flooded out of their homes and businesses, needless to say it was a challenging situation bordering on chaos.

Our offices fortunately remained dry throughout the storm, but the only way to physically reach them was by boat. Those companies that found their offices underwater—with supplies, furnishings, computer equipment, and records destroyed—had to find a new location, obtain new equipment, and begin rebuilding.

In the end, we were closed for about a week, during which we were unable to bill client businesses and collect revenue. For a specialty staffing company, that's significant. Cash flow became a real issue, because even when we were back up and running, many clients were struggling to recover. The time that it took for accounts to be paid almost doubled. What looked like a short-term problem became a longer-term issue. We had to make decisions on how to work with clients: What do we do with those firms that were so severely impacted by the storm that they may not survive? In the end, many did not survive, and that had a significant impact on us.

But in the midst of the devastation, something wondrous happened. The entire city of Houston came together to turn ruin into rescue and then recovery. The spirit was one of giving and generosity. Everyone, it seemed, knew someone who was having a worse go of it. Sterling Staffing Solutions and our other brands joined with many individuals and businesses to regain our beloved home. We served food to the homeless, organized food drives, prepared bags of clothes and blankets for shelters, and collected funds for employees or contractors who were impacted and needed to rebuild their homes. We also joined in Habitat for Humanity builds to help people who were impacted by Hurricane Harvey.

As we helped those impacted by Hurricane Harvey and found our footing again as a company, we realized that we were more than fortunate. We discovered that we had finally arrived: we had built a company strong enough to withstand a disaster the size of a thousand-year storm.

Harvey confirmed that we were on the right track in fulfilling the reason we had gone into business in the first place. We had formed Sterling Staffing Solutions to make a difference—for our families, our employees, our customers, and the community. Thanks to our beliefs in planning, organizing, having a strong work ethic, and being servant leaders, we had made good decisions that helped us grow from a company of one person with one phone to more than eight hundred people providing care in four states. And we are just getting started.

How It All Started

When people look at our company today, they see what appears to be a perfectly run operation that has prevailed against the odds in a tough marketplace, a company led by two entrepreneurs who have worked harmoniously to achieve success in a relatively short time. True, as twin brothers we have a closeness that few other partners in business share. But our success wasn't without trials and tribulations—like Hurricane Harvey—and it took dedication, perseverance, optimism, and vision for us to be where we are today.

We were fortunate enough to have discovered a niche in which to operate. That created a pathway for success. Our niche: staffing physical therapists in the home health industry.

We started Sterling Staffing Solutions because there was a high demand for physical therapists in the home health environment, a need we discovered when Sterling Physical Therapy and Wellness—the impetus for our current staffing company—received calls from physical therapists looking for work and calls from home health agencies needing therapists. Physical therapy was one of the fastest growing occupations at the time, and the home health industry was booming as well. The industry as a whole was changing because of the growing needs of the aging population and the rising costs of health care—patients were leaving the hospital after a three-day stay with a hefty $80,000 in medical bills. That began a push to help patients go home faster and receive care there.

That's how the Sterling Staffing Solutions niche was discovered.

Before opening the doors of our specialty staffing agency, we did our research to look at the possibilities and opportunities, and obtained a mentor to help us avoid common mistakes. Although we're twins and close brothers, that didn't necessarily mean we would be able to work well together. But our strengths complement each other, allowing us to harness the positive attributes of each partner and achieve greater results in a shorter period of time.

After much consideration, family discussion, and prayer, Sterling Staffing Solutions opened in 2011. Since the Sterling Physical Therapy and Wellness brand was already a commodity known for quality and attention to details, we decided to leverage the "Sterling" name with the new business.

The staffing company opened with one employee working remotely from home and the two of us still working in our separate fields—health care and oil and gas, respectively. In order to have the appropriate oversight of the business, we had to establish different software packages and communication tools that would allow us to monitor the business and react quickly when needed. Using cloud-based databases, online portals, text messages, emails, and chat rooms, we were able to communicate quickly and efficiently. That early virtual setup for the staffing company was the catalyst for the technology-driven remote model that we continue to use today. Since contract therapists don't do their work in the office—they work in health care facilities or in patients' homes—we operate in a largely remote capacity, enabled by technology.

We hired our first office-based employee in 2012 to man a separate phone line that, even then, was located in the physical therapy practice. After a few bumps in the road, we found our rhythm and the company began to grow—fast. We moved the company into its first office in 2013, and three years later, it outgrew that office and needed to move again. As the company grew, it became increasingly difficult for us to manage both the business and our full-time jobs. The outpatient clinic was growing, which took away from the time Sterling had to commit to the staffing company, and Stephen was burning the midnight oil just to stay afloat in both his passion at Sterling Staffing Solutions and his job in the oil and gas industry. Finally, both of us committed full time to the staffing company, leading to explosive growth in just a few years.

Today, the staffing company has taken off and we're expanding into other types of staffing and other areas of the country. If you're like us—if you are someone with a passion who wants to work for yourself in a business that makes money and succeeds—then start by finding your niche.

Finding Your Niche

According to the US Small Business Administration, small businesses comprise 99.7 percent of companies in the United States.[3] In 2014, that was more than 5.8 million companies according to US Census Bureau data.[4] That's a lot of competition.

Starting a company by trying to do the same thing as another company—going after the same customers in the same market with virtually the same product—will compound the other challenges you will face as a start-up. Instead, with all the options available to consumers today, finding a niche can help set you and your product apart.

Some of the world's biggest success stories started by targeting a very small niche. Tech companies alone are notorious for having been started in a garage with next to nothing in resources—Apple,

Hewlett-Packard, Amazon, and Google, to name four of the giants that have had tremendous influence on our lives.

But even if you don't set out to become the next Fortune 100 company, there's no reason you can't find a niche that will let you fulfill your dream of owning a business. Start by looking at the needs and interests where you live, and then consider these key points:

- Products and services: What need is going unfulfilled in my neighborhood? My community?

- Target audience or customers: Who would most likely want or need my product or service?

- Business model: How can I fill that need?

- Price point: How much can I charge for my goods and services?

If everyone tells you that you're a great baker, and you determine your niche is a cupcake shop, you must first determine whether the area you want to operate in already has more than its share of cupcake shops. Then you must figure out whether you even have the customer base—if you're eyeing a building across from a university, are there already ten other coffee and cupcake shops surrounding the campus? If so, then your niche may be a different operating model—maybe a roving cupcake stand or cupcakes delivered to the dorm room. That's all before you even begin considering how much to charge for each of your tasty treats.

Finding a niche or opportunity for a business may be as simple as pursuing something that interests you—a hobby, for instance. There's a lot to be said for doing what you love, and that's something that people will recognize when they become a customer. So if you're a model train buff, what's to stop you from starting an online trade shop?

If you don't have a real passion that seems to fill a niche, then start doing your homework. Niches are often found in industries that are constantly under change—such as technology or health care.

The internet is a great source for researching potential opportunities for a business start-up. Your local universities, business organizations, and even industry trade groups are other sources of good ideas.

If you're still stuck for ideas, start looking inward: Why do you want to be in business for yourself? The answer may come from figuring out exactly what drives you every day. Spend some time reflecting on what you do especially well. Ask people who know you well for input—people who are close enough to give you an honest, non-biased opinion. Take that constructive feedback and analyze it. Then once you determine what you're good at, focus on amplifying those positive aspects.

Find Your "Why"

Everyone needs to find what they're passionate about. In business, that can simply make it easier to go to work every day. But more than that, it can define what you do on a personal and professional level every day. Once you know your purpose—your "why"—it can guide everything you do. Thought leader Simon Sinek developed the concept of knowing your "why," which is, "the purpose, cause or belief that inspires you."[5]

> *Once you know your purpose—your
> "why"—it can guide everything you do.*

People often start their own company doing what they know best. On some level, for many, that's their "why"—they're branching out on their own because they love what they do and they are good at it, but they're working for a company whose values do not align with their own. They feel they have better values, and they want the world to benefit from them. They are driven to be leaders who not only captain their own ship but also serve people.

In fact, that was our shared "why." In our community, we don't have enough leaders—we don't have enough individuals operating businesses. When we formed Sterling Staffing Solutions, we wanted a company that would positively impact our families, our staff, and our community as a whole.

We decided early on that just having a health care staffing company in Houston was not enough. We wanted to be in every state. We wanted to operate and help people around the world. That's how we started this business, and that's what brought us to where we are today. We knew that putting our minds and our hearts into our idea, planning well, and working hard would help us achieve those dreams.

From the start, we also wanted our staffing agency to show others that they can succeed as well, that they can go beyond the status quo with more than just an eight-to-five job. We wanted our success to show others that anything is possible with the right motivation—the right niche and the right why.

While we shared the "desire to succeed despite the odds" as our business why, our personal whys were on different tracks. Yet, a clear understanding of each other's personal drivers allowed for our business and personal whys to blend quite nicely.

OUR PERSONAL WHYS

Dr. Sterling L. Carter

Twenty-five years of military experience gave me the opportunity to see the world, to experience different cultures and different situations. It also made me realize that no one is invincible. There is no guarantee for any individual that they will be here tomorrow—that made me realize at a very early age how precious life is.

When I first became a US Army combat medic at age nineteen, I knew even then that health care was my passion. Health care is a profession that's all about helping others, about making a positive difference in someone's life. That's been my "why" since day one. I'm a people person, and someone who is concerned about the happiness and well-being of others. Health care lets me provide a positive service to individuals—that helps them and, in turn, rewards me by knowing I made a difference. That's why I pursued physical therapy after returning from Operation Desert Storm, finishing my degree in two years. Afterward, I began working at a VA hospital. Although that job had good pay and benefits, and I stayed there for ten years, I wanted an opportunity to impact even more people. That's what the entrepreneurial world offers, so I left the VA and opened my own clinic.

The military also teaches you to complete the mission. That's what Stephen and I have always done. From finishing college after returning from war, to organizing, planning, and following through in our staffing company, we know that it takes that kind of drive and discipline to achieve great things.

Stephen Levi Carter

My dream was to be an independent business mogul—that has really been my "why." Even though I worked for years in the corporate world, I always wanted to succeed in business myself. Every bit of knowledge that I gathered from corporate America was always meant to be leveraged in my entrepreneurial pursuits. I earned a degree in accounting but found out that my personality and outlook on life was stifled in this field. Although I had a health care background from my US Army days, I gravitated toward oil and gas because of the vast opportunities in Houston and the appealing compensation. After getting an MBA, I returned briefly to health care working for a consulting firm. But soon enough, I returned to oil and gas, where I discovered I had a talent for the big picture side of finance and technology. That led to numerous opportunities, including a merger that supplied the cash allowing us to start the staffing agency.

On some level, I've always been an entrepreneur. Our mother was a great role model—beyond teaching, she was a real estate broker, a travel agent, and she even owned a snow cone stand when we were kids. She showed us the value of always having some sort of entrepreneurial activity going, some way of working for ourselves. She always wanted us to define our own destiny.

So, like our mother, I've always had that entrepreneurial drive. My business interests and investments over the years have included a digital publishing platform, a public relations and promotions company, a beauty and grooming studio, an upscale restaurant, and a full-service accounting and tax consulting firm. All of those different experiences taught me what to do and what not to do before starting Sterling Staffing Solutions.

Sinek suggests looking at your entire life to discover your "why." Think of five to seven different stories that stand out to you, good or bad. Memorable things that have happened that changed your life, from childhood to adulthood. Then tell your story to someone who isn't biased—someone other than a parent or a spouse. Tell them the stories that shaped you as a person, and as you do, look for patterns and messages that stand out. Those collectively can help you determine your "why." You'll be amazed to discover how the different memorable activities in your life have shaped you into the person you are—how they are the reason for doing what you do.

Why Are You in Business?

Once you know what motivates you and made you the person you are, convert that into the "why" for your company. Aligning your personal and professional "why"s makes it much easier to be authentic when sharing your vision for the company—your passion, commitment, and confidence in your company will come through as you tell your story.

If your business structure involves a partnership, then each partner's "why" must be aligned to have the buy-in needed to move the company forward.

Purpose and passion also drive the formation of the "why" for the business. Often described as mission, values, or purpose statements, these must be simple and concise in order to be effective and to obtain buy-in.

When we created the mission for Sterling Staffing Solutions, we wanted to develop a holistic, motivational mindset that would inspire our team. We wanted to ensure that the mission addressed our patients, our clinicians, our clients, and our community. We didn't want to address just the "what," but also the "how." In other words, we wanted our mission statement to have some accountability built in. Finally, we required buy-in from our team so that they would embrace and live the mission daily.

We spent weeks developing the mission statement. We engaged our management team and staff along the way, and we even asked for external feedback from our clients and clinicians. Here is what we came up with:

STERLING STAFFING SOLUTIONS MISSION

*To exceed the expectations of our patients
and their loved ones.*

*To support our clinicians in a way that
respects their talent and encourages their
professional growth and autonomy.*

*To foster meaningful partnerships with our clients,
producing a more profitable and sustainable
business model than ever imagined.*

*To enhance the communities in which we
operate by employing local talent and
investing in the areas where we work.*

It's easy when formulating mission and value statements to believe that once the words are on paper, you're done, but that's not the way it works. If you truly want your employees to live and breathe and understand the values of your company, then *you* must live and breathe them every day. For instance, our mission is posted on the reception wall of the office so that everyone that walks through the door sees it. We also start every meeting reiterating our "why" for being in business, our "why" for following this calling. And the company fulfills its "why" by staffing out high-level, high-skilled health care providers to patients in need.

Employees need to know that the leaders of a company are not just in business for the money. It's not just about the owners trying to make millions of dollars to buy a nice house and drive a nice car. It's about your purpose, your vision, your mission. Once the team buys into that vision, it can really take on its own identity. It can serve as a beacon for the team, helping them work together toward that singular mission, that singular goal.

We learned that in our military training—having everyone on board as a team to accomplish one goal. In the military, that goal was to protect a nation, and that all-for-one mindset has served us very well in our company. With our remote business model, it is crucial to have that kind of team spirit and vision for the company.

Once you understand your purpose—your vision, your mission, your "why"—amplify those positive attributes and use them to move your company forward. Do that, and you'll find that it's very difficult for you to fail, because clients that understand and align with your "why" will want to do business with you.

In a nutshell, your first steps are:

1.   **Find your niche.**

2.   **Discover your "why."**

3.   **Align your "why" and your niche, so that your staff and customers buy into your vision.**

With your niche and your "why" determined, it's time to vet your idea and be willing to put in the work to make it come to fruition.

Is There Any "There" There?

People who dream of going into business for themselves often start their venture based purely on the idea that they have what they believe is a unique, earth-shattering concept. They know in their heart that their idea will be a raging success, so they push forward without analyzing the market or doing any research to know whether the idea will really fly. When the idea fails—after much effort and expense—of course, they're disappointed. But all that could have been avoided with the right research up front.

Before we opened the doors of our staffing company, we spent an extensive amount of time researching the business, looking at the demographics, the competition, and other factors that would play into the company's success. Even though we felt that we had evidence of a niche, our goal in doing so much homework up front was to determine whether that niche was real.

As a result, the staffing company's success has not been by accident. There was a defined plan from the start.

We started by searching for answers to the basics of business— the simple concept of supply and demand: How many other staffing companies are out there? How many of them fill health care positions? Who are their customers? Are there any unmet needs? Then we delved deeper: What kind of quality do they deliver? How are they structured? What do they typically charge per visit?

Then we asked the big question: What can we do to make us different? When looking to fill a niche, you may find that other companies in the marketplace already have offerings the same as or similar to your idea. It doesn't make sense to open a new business if there aren't enough customers to go around, especially in an over-saturated market. But it can be done if you figure out your differentiator: What is going to set your business apart from others? That differentiator may be simply a matter of delivering better quality.

What is going to set your business apart from others?

Since we wanted to focus on home health, we needed to ensure that we were operating in an area that had a lot of home health agencies that we could market to. We also needed an area with a large elderly population, since home health agencies largely serve people sixty-five and older, on Medicare or Medicaid, often with disabilities.

We looked into the specific needs in the home health environment, and we quickly determined that there was a limited supply of physical therapists willing to do home health care and a very high demand for these clinicians in this area. We decided very quickly that our niche would be to provide physical therapists to home health agencies in order to take care of their patients at home.

Once we launched in our niche market and things were going well, we reassessed to determine how we could outperform our competition (other therapy staffing companies). We wanted to know how big they were and what they were doing that we could do better. We found that a lot of staffing companies only offered physical therapy or occupational therapy. *Bingo.* Our niche would be as a one-stop shop. We would provide all the home health needs: physical therapy, occupational therapy, speech therapy, social work, and, in time, even nursing.

We also recognized very quickly in our research that health care administration is still very much an antiquated industry. Paper files, fax machines, handwritten forms. We knew we could stand out from the crowd if we used our tech-savviness to improve operations. We incorporated an electronic medical record system into our plan that allowed us to be almost completely paperless. It allowed us to have e-signatures and to communicate with staff via text, email, or fax.

In short, we carefully and thoughtfully started the company after doing a ton of research on how to make it successful. We determined that we needed to have a nimble, efficient, and low-cost model that would allow us to contract with a lot of therapists and have them see a lot of patients, all while watching the bottom line and maintaining our profits.

That's what it means to determine whether there is any "there" there. Before opening the doors to any business, you must first figure out whether your idea will hold water.

Measure Twice, Cut Once

There's an old, yet still relevant, adage often used in the construction industry that certainly applies also to business planning: measure twice, cut once.

Even if you have an idea that seems to fill a niche, you must still vet that idea. You must look at your market and decide whether your idea will really fly: Where are your customers? What problem is your product solving? Who is your competition? How sustainable is your idea?

Getting the answers to these questions and more is going to require some research. No matter how much you're in love with your own idea, you must have proof. Even if everyone tells you what a great cook you are, that doesn't mean you should open your own kitchen in a building where three restaurants have already failed. You may have friends over every weekend raving about your great barbecue, but will they drive to your new diner, bring their friends, and actually pay you for a meal? Why did three restaurants already fail? Those are the kinds of hard questions you have to ask and answer.

And then of course there are the money questions: How much do you charge for the product or service? How are you going to fund this million-dollar idea? Finances can limit almost any new business in really getting off the ground, and in growing later. So where is the start-up money coming from?

These questions and others can be answered by putting together a business plan. A business plan can help you determine whether you have a viable idea while helping to lay out the steps to start your venture. There are some very good business planning software options available, many of which have research tools that lead you through the steps to put your plan together. Some of the software options are industry specific; research the best for your needs by looking for consumer reviews and ratings online.

LivePlan is a very good business planning software program. There are also some very good reviews about various software programs on Business.com—just enter "business planning software" in the search bar.

LivePlan is a very good business planning software program. There are also some very good reviews about various software programs on Business.com—just enter "business planning software" in the search bar.

Technology today puts innumerable options for researching your ideas at your fingertips. You can conduct online searches about your industry, your competition, demographics, and even pricing for your product or service.

There are also numerous government websites available. The Small Business Administration (SBA) has a wealth of reliable information available to help start-ups. From business guides to funding programs to links for local assistance from mentors or development programs, the SBA is a great place to start learning what you need to know to be a business owner. We also found the Census Bureau site to be a great resource for understanding the demographics of the area we were targeting. Census data is public knowledge and is broken down by city, county, state, and more.

Check out these sites for start-ups:

US Small Business Administration
www.sba.gov

US Census Bureau
www.census.gov

US Chamber of Commerce
www.uschamber.com

Starting a new business may also mean finding out details such as whether you need a license to operate or to employ certain skill sets—information best learned before opening the doors. Licenses may be covered by federal, state, or local rules. For instance, health care is a heavily regulated industry, and licenses are required for any business or person that provides hands-on care. But that is public information, so we were able to obtain a list of addresses and contact information from the Texas Department of Aging and Disability Services for all the licensed home health agencies in the state.

Also look up local business organizations and publications. Your local chamber of commerce, or the chamber where you want to operate, should be ready and willing to either give you the help you need or refer you somewhere for answers. Industry trade organizations can also connect you with statistics, insights, and even mentors who can help you obtain the answers you need.

Don't forget your area universities—often there are programs to help entrepreneurs turn their ideas into real businesses.

In our case, since we were particularly interested in the issues the other home health agencies had with staffing companies, our research included picking up the phone and making some calls. Don't be afraid to do that kind of due diligence to find out what your potential customers are looking for in a newcomer to the market.

These measures represent just a sampling of the kind of in-depth research we did before starting a staffing agency, even though we knew there was a market because of all the calls that the clinic had already been receiving.

In short, do your homework. Let your passion drive you. And stick with it. The more information you can gather, the better your decisions can be.

Goals: Marks of Achievement

Researching your idea can also help you begin to formulate what your company will look like. One of the best ways to achieve your dreams is to set goals for the business. With goals set, you always have a new mark to reach for, a new win to achieve.

One of the best ways to achieve your dreams is to set goals for the business. With goals set, you always have a new mark to reach for, a new win to achieve.

When setting goals, many people go with the familiar SMART goals idea, which states that goals must be (s)pecific, (m)easurable, (a)ttainable, (r)elevant, and (t)imely. But we've gone one step further—with **BE SMARTER** goals: (b)uild in accountability, (e)xamine as you go, (s)pecify and stagger, (m)easure for progress, (a)ttainability is key, (r)elevant to you and your team, (t)ime sensitive, (e)ye on the prize, and (r)each for something more.

Build in Accountability

When creating goals, build in accountability to help ensure that goals stay on track. For instance, put the goals in writing, then share them with others. Once others know what each member of the team is responsible for, it's easier to hold everyone accountable.

Examine As You Go

It's easy to become caught up in the day-to-day running of a business; before you know it, your goal deadline is here and you've done nothing toward reaching it. Take time every day—or once a week at minimum—to examine where you are with your goals. We sit down at a prescheduled time twice a week to talk about the projects we're working on and how close we are to achieving those goals.

Specify and Stagger

Your goals should specify what you aim to accomplish by answering six w's:

1. *Who should be involved in achieving the goal?*

2. *What are the specifics of the goal?*

3. *When do you anticipate completion of the goal? (See more under "Time Sensitive," below.)*

4. *Where are the key locations the goal is to be achieved?*

5. *Why is this goal important?*

6. *Which resources are needed to complete the goal?*

To keep the momentum going year over year, stagger the end dates of your goals—short and long term—and then set a new goal as each is completed, like building blocks of achievement. If your goal is to make $2 million in revenue, make that your long-term goal, and set attainable short-term goals to achieve that larger goal. For instance, quarterly goals could help you feel like you're realistically on the way to that $2 million figure.

Measure for Progress

Any goal worth achieving is worth measuring. By measuring your progress toward your goals, you can virtually move the dial on your company. Measures might include specific dates for completion, more income, or cost savings. A goal with defined parameters such as, "Reduce costs by 10 percent in six months," is easier to measure than one saying, "We must cut corners somewhere."

Attainability is Key

Start with short-term goals that are easy wins, something to keep the team interested and always looking ahead. And be realistic about the goal. Doubling your business might be doable when you're a start-up—after all, if you start with two customers and then add two more, you've just experienced 100 percent growth, right? But trying to keep up that kind of year-over-year percentage will only leave you and your team discouraged. (It can be far tougher to add two thousand new customers in a single year.)

Relevant to You and Your Team

It is more difficult to drive a team to succeed when formulating goals that are not aligned with your company's "why."

Time Sensitive

In addition to a deadline for completing a goal, also create a timeline for achieving steps along the way.

Eye On the Prize

Like a kid in a candy store, it's easy to become a little too eager when it comes to creating goals. As a business owner, there may be times when you want it all and you want it now. But especially when starting out, limit the number of goals you set at one time—no more than three to five long-term goals at once. That can help you and the team stay focused on the prize.

Reach for Something More

Stretch or long-term goals set the vision for the company to be a huge success. They push you and your company to the limits by serving as a constant source of inspiration. They keep people dreaming of bigger and better instead of falling into a pattern of complacency.

Finally, we have one additional tip for setting goals: *encourage input from the team.* You may have heard of the Toyota model of continuous improvement, which involves investing heavily in the team and gaining input from everyone—from executives to workers on the shop floor—a model to be admired, certainly.

We believe in communicating opportunities to the team. In setting goals, it's important to gain as much input from the team as we can, because the team members are the ones out there doing the work every day. We like to bring ideas to the table, but start by brainstorming with the team to bounce around ideas until we come up with workable solutions.

When goal setting with the team, keep this in mind: don't hit them with too much too soon. Too many goals, too much change at once, can be overwhelming and ultimately lower morale.

Take Action

Once your goals are set, it's time to begin taking action. That means creating steps to achieve the goals. Assign the goals to individuals so that everyone understands their part in achieving them. Then dedicate time every day to the goals and make sure you're checking off those items.

For example, if your goal is to double the amount of sales, just sharing the goal with your staff won't take you very far. Instead, it must be broken down into action steps for each member of the team. Otherwise, the way Mindy in human resources interprets a doubling of sales will be different than how Sam in accounting does.

The goals must be specific to each person so that, for example, someone in human resources can understand how X number of people must be recruited on a monthly basis while the salespeople understand that they must close X number of new clients each month for the company to reach its goals.

To help us with goal setting, we live and die by a vision board—a whiteboard we've posted on the wall at the main office. It's there for us to see every day to remind us to stay on track.

On the board, we list the action items in line with our short- and long-term goals. The items are broken down into manageable steps that cover shorter time periods: day by day, week by week, and month by month. These steps are constantly updated to keep us on target with our goals.

THE MORNING VISION BOARD—BY STEPHEN LEVI CARTER, MBA

I'm such a fan of vision boards that I literally start my day with one. Using dry erase markers, I write out the goals for the year on my morning mirror. Then every morning, when I'm getting ready for the day, I see those goals.

The idea has really caught on in my family. My wife sees my goals every morning, adding an extra layer of accountability for me, and my kids now put their goals on their mirror as well, giving them something to strive for every day.

My morning vision board has helped crystallize for my family what it is I'm working toward every day, and has helped engage them in the process.

Setting goals and obtaining them can be two vastly different things. Many people are good at setting goals but fail miserably when it comes to accomplishing them. Really, setting a goal and accomplishing that goal is like painting a picture. Artists typically set out to paint something that in the end will be beautiful, memorable, and valuable, but first they must come up with a concept, choose the paint medium, design the color scheme, and determine the timeline for completing the project.

Setting goals and obtaining them can be two vastly different things.

Vincent Van Gogh, arguably the greatest painter in history, was an exceptional talent who had his own distinctive and spontaneous style. Van Gogh was a Dutch post-impressionist painter who is among the most famous and influential figures in Western art. In just over a decade he created approximately 2,100 works of art, most of which were completed in the last two years of his life. Van Gogh described the process for his work as follows:

> *"The work is an absolute necessity for me. I can't put it off, I don't care for anything but the work; that is to say, the pleasure in something else ceases at once and I become melancholy when I can't go on with my work. Then I feel like a weaver who sees that his threads are tangled, and the pattern he had on the loom is gone to hell, and all his thought and exertion is lost."[6]*

Like Van Gogh, you must have a laser-like commitment to completing your goals. We've used a step process over the years that we call ARTIST, which we have found brings us consistent results in reaching goals:

Activities | Resources | Total Costs | Indicators | Sequence | Timeline

Activities.

Identify each of the activities required to meet the goal.

Resources.

Determine the resources needed for each activity—whether a person, a team, a leader, or an outside resource.

Total costs.

Identify costs associated with each activity. Do you need new equipment, marketing collateral, more labor hours, more personnel? For us, communicating with our contractor base more efficiently meant developing a new system that would also save on internal staff time. That may sound like a big expenditure, but investing in the right software package actually cut our labor costs overall because we no longer have to spend so much time on manual tasks.

Indicators.

Define the key performance indicators (KPIs), the metrics that are set for each person on the team, each department in the company. By hitting those KPIs month after month, the company can and will grow—and reach its goal.

Sequence.

Create a sequence of events. Some activities will rely on others being done first.

Timeline.

Create the timeline for achieving the goal. Don't just set start and end points. Be sure to stop at predetermined points to measure the action plan's progress. The worst thing you can do is create goals, implement an action plan, and then wait until the deadline to look at the activity and see where you are in achieving your goal. If the goal is set for six months out, then check the progress of it every month. If the plan is not progressing as it should, then those checkpoints give you a chance to retool the plan, reassign resources and tasks, and reassess the value of the activity.

Once you've created your detailed action plan, it's time to implement it—beginning by clearly communicating the goals to excite the team and obtain their buy-in. As the leader, you can have as many goals or big ideas as you want, but until you communicate them effectively to every rank of the organization and engage the team, you won't have anyone to help move the ball forward.

As you're defining your goals and creating your action plan, think about efficiencies. For example, a high-level goal like doubling the size of the business in a single year may not mean doubling expenses. With each step of your goal setting and action planning, ask: How can we do more business with less? You may not have what you need on hand, so you'll have to decide whether the costs of building at point A to take you to point Z are justified. You may have to be creative in your planning: Is outsourcing or even renting equipment a good solution for the short or long term? And as CEO, where does it make the most sense—cost- and value-wise—to be spending your time?

Another component in action planning is identifying your risks and hurdles. For instance, if quality is important to your business and there is the potential for quality to suffer along the way, then decisions about how to prevent that lapse in quality need to be made up front.

Quality is so important to us that, when we decided to double our business, we wrote out our goals and held a big meeting to discuss them with the team. When the team members arrived, they were met with a slideshow that included the image of a bucket with holes in it. To demonstrate our point about quality, the slides showed water being poured into the bucket and then shooting out the holes as fast as the bucket was filled.

The more water that went in, the more that came out—there was no way to fill the bucket fast enough to get ahead of the drainage. The idea was to give the team a visual to help explain our concept of quality: It doesn't matter how hard we work to double our business if we're not maintaining quality. It doesn't matter how many clients we land if we're not keeping those clients happy. In fact, if our quality suffers, we could end up losing more clients than we gain. So for us, part of goal setting and action planning must always include identifying how to maintain quality and keep it from suffering as we grow.

Be Organized from the Start

As you can see by now, starting out in business takes some real organization—and that's something to be done from day one.

In the military, training breaks everything down to the lowest common denominator. Green recruits are going to be put behind high-powered weapons, so there must be processes in place that can move everyone from A to Z very quickly.

That same value exists in business: Your organization will operate more smoothly if you build policies and processes that anyone can walk into. Ironing out and writing down standard operating policies and procedures eliminates mistakes, improves quality, and creates efficiencies. Investing so much up front will save time, energy, and effort down the road.

You cannot assume that everyone who works for you knows exactly what to do in any situation. In fact, you have to assume that they don't. It's useful to have formal policies in place to create structure for people to follow, especially with the reality of employee turnover. You may have a staffer who is great at answering phones—they are professional, and they know what to say and not to say. But if you have to replace that person, you'll be glad you have written procedures in place. Formal, written telephone policies can cover everything from how to announce your business to never saying "I don't know."

At our company, our policy states that "I don't know" is replaced with "I don't have the answer right now, but I can research that and find out for you." Formal policies help develop habits in our staff and let them know what to do in any situation.

When putting together your policies, remember that everyone doesn't learn the same way. Some people can read a manual and they're good to go, while others need to be trained hands-on. For others still, a video is best. Use a variety of methods when setting up your policies and processes. We have training manuals, videos, and checklists, and we do role-playing to help our staff know exactly what they should and shouldn't do in their role.

THE POWER OF POLICIES
by Dr. Sterling L. Carter

Everything in the military is set on structure. Everyone is supposed to follow the rules. When they do, things tend to turn out well. When they don't, things tend to end with disaster.

In 1991, I was serving as a combat medic in the 142nd Field Artillery Unit in the Persian Gulf. The unit's job was to fire over the infantry from Howitzer tanks to create as much damage as possible in a preassigned area and reduce risk for the foot soldiers who would then go in and clear out the damaged area.

At one point, we were in a convoy transporting military weapons to the next area for clearing—one long line of military vehicles traveling along a road. Since it was combat territory, anything off the road was not necessarily safe. Hazards all along the roadside included land mines and unexploded bombs that had been dropped from planes.

At times, the convoy halted for up to half an hour, because stop-and-go is how a line of fifty such vehicles moves. During those stops, some soldiers would step out of the vehicles and look for souvenirs to take home—money or weapons or what have you—but it was against the policies and procedures to do so. No one was supposed to be picking up anything in an unsafe area.

During one of those stops, a soldier left his vehicle and picked up a shiny tube, then began swinging it around from the string that was hanging off one end. The other occupant of his vehicle was just saying "Don't bring it over here," when the object struck the vehicle—and exploded. Luckily, no one was killed, but the soldier who had picked up the device lost his hand, and the soldier in the vehicle lost his eyesight from flying shrapnel.

That one act of not following procedure completely changed two lives forever.

As a highly regulated industry involved in hands-on patient care, policies and procedures are crucial in health care. Yet, health care is constantly changing. On the clinical side, what is protocol today may be a different protocol tomorrow. On the administrative side, guidelines are changing to address fraud, improve standards of care, and cut costs. Policies and procedures must keep up with all this—we have to be nimble enough to make changes on the fly. It goes beyond just ensuring that changes are communicated to staff; it's also making sure everyone is accountable.

As the business leader, you must be willing to change with the times—you cannot be averse to change. That goes for employees also, which means they must be given the autonomy to make changes as needed to improve processes and make your company more efficient. The most earth-shattering changes that make the biggest difference often come from the field, the people who are doing the hands-on work with products or clients. These employees must be empowered to let their ideas flow, and those ideas that improve the company should be incorporated.

Up-front research and start-up planning are effective in any industry, and once the model is set, it can be used to diversify the company. When you've reached the point of growth and are ready to look for opportunities, start by looking for those that are very similar to what you're already doing, those that add high value but don't take up a significant amount of time. For example, we started off staffing physical therapists, then occupational therapists. Then we realized there was a need to staff speech therapists, so we began offering those clinicians to our clients. Same organizational model, just a different discipline. Then we went into social work, then registered nurses, then medical doctors.

If you can diversify within your discipline, you can gain a broader target audience. Your company becomes much more marketable, because you can do more without spreading your bandwidth too far. That's how we captured the market in health care.

A word of caution: Be careful when diversifying. If you try to do too much or spread yourself too thin, you can reach a point where you're a "master of none."

When you begin to diversify, you may also run into some pushback. But if you're going to be a nimble organization, you can't have people on board who are opposed to change.

Overcoming the Naysayers

Society has taught us that we're supposed to go to school, earn a college degree, land a job, work fifty-plus years, and then retire. You buy your house, start a family, get a dog, and put up a white picket fence, and that's called success. But for an entrepreneur or someone who owns or wants to own a business, it's a completely different mind-set. It's walking away from stability, taking a risk, and not really knowing what the future may hold.

When you're someone who wants more than the status quo, you already see the world through a different lens—so at the end of the day, you must trust your gut, because there will always be someone out there who doesn't see the world the way you do. They're doing what works for them.

In pursuit of a goal, there will be naysayers along the way, including family and close friends. The world is not without its share of people who won't see your vision, who won't understand what you're trying to do and what you're trying to build.

Now, don't surround yourself with nothing but yes-men, people who won't give you any pushback at all. But you also don't want only people at the other end of the spectrum—people who are always negative, have nothing good to add, and are so rigid that they can't see your vision.

It is good to have people with different perspectives to challenge your thinking, people who have ideas to add positive changes that improve whatever you're trying to do. But you don't need people who just want to challenge you because they don't understand the risks you're willing to take.

In fact, some people even use negativity as fuel to keep pushing through. If you're like us, you saw your share of bullying in school. But you know that it ultimately made you resilient—it made you more aware that others won't always respect you, and that you can succeed in spite of what others think. That same type of mentality has to take place when you're in the business environment. You can almost use the naysaying as fuel to develop an "I'll show you" attitude. If you're in business for the right reasons, just develop tunnel vision and keep your focus and don't let anyone steer you astray.

To combat naysaying, listen to what others in business or in your industry have to say. There are podcasts and books and blogs shared by others who are going through the same thing you are. It doesn't matter what type of business; everyone has had to deal with something similar to your situation. Aligning yourself with like minds can soften the blows; knowing that you're not alone can be empowering.

Finally, recognize that one of the biggest naysayers might be the one inside you. Entrepreneurship can be a lonely venture, filled with self-doubt. When that happens, have faith in yourself. If you have a strong spiritual connection, look to that for strength—have faith in a higher power to guide you.

If you're leaving a corporate job, then go all in. Don't live with one foot in and one foot out. Give 150 percent to your venture—as much as you gave your corporate job and more—if you truly want to succeed.

DON'T LOOK BACK
by Stephen Levi Carter, MBA

If you're in corporate America today, it can be a big decision to leave a steady paycheck, benefits, and the perceived sense of stability. One of my motivators was just proving the naysayers wrong. I wanted others to see that it is possible to make it on your own.

When I finally decided to leave corporate America and take on the role of CEO of Sterling Staffing Solutions full time, I did so because I realized that fulfilling the dream meant wholeheartedly believing in it. If I didn't believe in it, why was I involved at all?

So I took the leap even though it was a sacrifice financially. With a family, home mortgage, two car payments, day care costs, school loans, and credit card debt, I had the typical lifestyle that went along with a steady paycheck. It was a big decision for the family as a whole, but it has turned out to be the best decision I ever made. It took a belief that it was something we could do. I believed that if I put my heart and soul into it, we could really make this thing explode. The sense of accomplishment is indescribable. When you work for someone else, you have to get any validation of your good work from the management team. As an entrepreneur, your validation is the growth of your business and the lives that you touch.

Interestingly, once an entrepreneur or innovator achieves success, the naysayers along the way sometimes become the biggest supporters. You're applauded by people whose view of you and your dreams has changed. Sometimes what you're dealing with are simply early or late adopters. Early adopters are those who are with you from day one—they believe in your vision and want to see you or even help you succeed. Late adopters are those that lack the ability to see your vision or are too risk adverse to make the jump themselves. Since they don't believe they can make it in a venture of their own, they don't believe you can do it either.

Although more a form of flattery than of naysaying, there will also be those who see your success as a target. Once someone realizes that something you're doing has value, they may want the same for themselves and their business. So you might find yourself being mimicked by other companies that want to copy your business model and even go after your clients. At the same time, you may also gain a new group of critics, those who don't believe you deserve your success—who think you were just "lucky," and that otherwise you could not have made it in their city, their industry, their area of expertise.

Still, someone in the crowd may have been your biggest cheerleader all along, someone who believed in your vision. When building a company, you need people like that on board, people who can bring to the table things that you cannot. Those are the kind of people you can cultivate relationships with, leading to bigger and better things.

The Importance of Relationships

I t's been said that being in a marriage is easier than being a partner with someone in business. Since we are twins, we had a unique bond before going into business together that would seem to give us an edge over most partnerships. And yet working together as partners has not been completely without its challenges.

Still, for us, of all the business structures, a partnership made the most sense. More than our biological relationship, there were other advantages: When we began the staffing business, we were both already in management positions, our personalities complemented each other, and our experiences lent themselves to each taking on different roles in leading the company. Plus, as brothers and friends, we knew each other's strengths, weaknesses, and quirks, and could work with and around those.

Business partners spend a lot of time together—and in a start-up, that may be more time than with family. During all that time, some big decisions are made—big career-building or career-ending decisions. All those ups and downs can come with a lot of emotional upheaval, a lot of personal sacrifices.

That's why it makes sense to use your head—not your heart—when deciding on a business partner.

Use your head—not your heart—
when deciding on a business partner.

Merriam-Webster defines a partnership as "a legal relation existing between two or more persons contractually associated as joint principals in a business," and as "a relationship resembling a legal partnership and usually involving close cooperation between parties having specified and joint rights and responsibilities."[7] The latter of these holds a few keys to choosing a partner—"close cooperation," and "joint rights and responsibilities." Let's look at these and other traits to consider when choosing a partner.

Choosing a Partner

In the United States, more than half of marriages end in divorce.[8] That's roughly the lower end of the spectrum when it comes to estimates about how many partnerships fail—numbers point to anywhere from 50 to 80 percent.[9] While there's an entire industry devoted to counseling to save marriages, partners have far fewer resources when it's time to save the relationship. With so much at stake, rather than waiting until dissolution is on the horizon, do your homework up front to build a stronger partnership in the first place.

Here are some of the traits to look for when creating a working partnership for the long term. Consider these before putting together a partnership agreement.

A Blend of Complementing Experiences

Ideally, a partnership is made up of leaders who come from different but complementing experiences. Our partnership works well because of the blend of corporate management and health industry leadership.

Equal Level of Commitment

When one partner has a financial commitment while the other invests only sweat equity, over time the shared responsibility may feel unequal. That's because it's difficult to quantify sweat equity unless a wage is placed on it in advance in the partnership agreement.[10] Ideally, find a partner who can invest both time and funds into the business.

Credit Counts

Partners are responsible for the financials in a company, so the credit worthiness of each partner must be considered before an agreement is signed. If one partner has strong credit but the other does not, it can limit the access the business has to cash—financiers hesitate to loan or give lines of credit to companies whose partners have less than stellar personal credit. When considering potential partners, ask: Do they pay their bills on time? Do they have a lot of debt? Are they a risk taker or more conservative? Regardless of how much capital one person may bring to the relationship, credit is king in business.

Complementing Business Personalities

Rather than have two risk takers running the show, balance that by having a partner who makes decisions from an analytical and strategic perspective. While big-picture thinkers and visionaries are needed to move the dial in a business, it also takes leaders with a more methodical or systematic approach to help a business stay grounded. Having business personalities on both ends of the spectrum allows us to meet in the middle.

Look at the Long Term

One reason partnerships fail is that they came into existence with a short-term perspective. Too often, someone decides they need a partner and then grabs the first person who steps up—often because that person has start-up capital or is connected to a contract the company needs in order to get the business off the ground. But beyond that initial contribution, the person brings no other value to the company long term. Fast-forward a few years, and the result is a lot of frustration and resentment because profits are being shared with someone who is bringing in no present-day value.

Who Decides?

The number of partners and the roles they play may not always dictate the percentage of ownership. And percentage of ownership determines voting rights. For example, we are fifty/fifty partners, which works for us from both the ownership and voting standpoints. However, it takes agreement by both of us to move forward—if either of us votes no on a particular situation, the business doesn't advance. On the flip side, a fifty/fifty partnership can actually help overcome decision-making impasses, forcing compromise at times. Just like in a marriage, you won't win every argument as an entrepreneur and you must learn to pick your battles.

Still, in a business partnership, it may make sense to have one person with a bit more control, a tie-breaking percentage of ownership. Beware, however, of the three-partner arrangement, where two may gang up on the other, leaving one partner never having their way and ultimately ending up uncomfortable, frustrated, and even ready to leave the business.

Whatever the percentages of ownership, determine them up front as part of the partnership agreement.

Return on Investment

Any partnership should start with a "transparent, agreed-upon financial plan for money management."[11] That means determining what kind of return on investment the partners can expect. That may or may not factor sweat equity into the equation; regardless of the amount of work any one partner does over the others, each partner typically expects a share of the profits.[12]

Communication Is Key

With partnerships, communication is crucial. Regardless of the roles, partners must be able to communicate well, or else their lack of cohesiveness can infect the entire organization.

Making the Partnership Work

Considering the amount of time that partners spend together and all that is at stake, it's good to have some basic ideas about how to make a partnership work before getting in too deep. Here are some tips.

Divvy Up the Work

Remember, it's not about the title; it's about the roles. Consider what each partner brings to the table in the way of leadership skills. Some CEOs are strong in the money side of business, others in organization or in sales and marketing.

Before signing a partnership agreement, determine what roles each partner will assume. Ideally, strengths and weaknesses of the partners will create a productive balance in the organization.

Respect Ideas

Be open to ideas—and open to discussion. Just as in a marriage or any relationship, a partnership requires active listening. When one partner has an idea, listen and then process it before responding. Be respectful of partners' opinions and ask questions; don't just blurt out "no." In short, vet ideas before making a collective decision.

Recognize the Value of the Other Partner(s)

Even in the strongest partnerships—those based on very strategic decisions—partners will question the value of the relationship. When that happens, look back to the struggles that you've been through together and decide whether the bonds are still there. Is everyone still 100 percent invested in the partnership and in the best interests of the business?

As with any close relationship, a partnership will have its ups and downs. When you are tied to someone else in a business partnership, you must figure out how to work through those times when you question the other partner's direction or commitment. Remember the reason you went into business together in the first place—to build something that will make an impact for generations to come. In a good partnership, there will be plenty of moments when you realize that if it weren't for your partner, the business would have missed some great opportunities. It can be very expensive to leave a partnership, so choose wisely and then remember every day why you value your partner.

Keep Egos—And Expectations—In Check

Ego kills relationships. But keeping an ego in check can be especially tough for someone who has already had some success in the past.

Partners in a business are often lions—they're leaders, not followers. They're used to being the boss. That comes with a level of confidence—and can come with ego. But there's a difference between

Confidence is being open to what others have to say and having the self-assurance to drive the company forward. Ego is insisting that something is possible even when evidence proves otherwise; it's ignoring others and pushing ahead just to have your own way.

confidence and ego. Confidence is being open to what others have to say and having the self-assurance to drive the company forward. Ego is insisting that something is possible even when evidence proves otherwise; it's ignoring others and pushing ahead just to have your own way.

Unmet expectations can also cause tension in a business. If a goal is to make $20 million in one year, and a plan is followed but falls short, then any *expectations* that the goal would be met turn to disappointment and frustration. Keeping ego and expectations in check can keep operations on a more even keel.

Consider a Personality Assessment

When it comes to finding a partner—or building a team for your business—nothing beats a personality assessment. These can help determine whether a person is a good fit in personality and skill set.

For instance, you would not want a passive personality in your billings and collections department—you need someone who is more outspoken and assertive. Meanwhile, leaders need to be compassionate and understanding and yet steadfast—you don't want leaders who are indecisive or sway with every whim.

A couple of very good personality assessment tools include the Myers-Briggs Type Indicator, a self-reporting questionnaire that can reveal a person's personality and decision-making perspective.[13] The assessment, based on noted psychiatrist Carl Jung's theory of psychological type, identifies sixteen personality types and can reveal the combination of types that are dominant in an individual. Results of the assessment can help people understand and relate to each other.

Another assessment is known as DiSC.[14] Based on the work of psychologist William Moulton Marston, DiSC looks at four behavioral traits: (**d**)ominance, (**i**)nfluence, (**s**)teadiness, and (**c**)onscientiousness. DiSC is ideal for helping leaders understand how to better communicate with employees.

Communication Is Key

In the next principle, we'll discuss the value of good communication in greater depth. As it applies to communicating as a leader, one technique that we really like is the sandwich method, in which less-than-ideal news or information is "sandwiched" between good news—good news is presented first, then the less-than-ideal news, then finally good news again.

With communication between partners, ensure there are no secrets or surprises, especially when it comes to finances. The key to having a healthy and strong partnership is making sure partners never feel left out of the loop.

Discuss Major Financial Decisions with Each Other

When it comes to spending money, set a threshold for the big decisions. Obviously, you don't want the partners to be so confined that they can't make financial decisions on their own, but decide on a certain level of expenditure that must be approved by the partners or the board of directors. Group decision making on the financial information should also apply when setting up, say, a contract for ongoing services.

Hold Regular Meetings

We've mentioned how we hold regular meetings to ensure that everyone is on the same page and we're moving the dial on the company's goals. In those meetings, be sure to have an agreed-upon, written agenda to stay focused and keep the meeting on track. Also, avoid the temptation to skip a meeting; after the first one, missing a meeting gets easier and easier. Choose a standing block of time and put it on your calendar, and then stick to it—don't let anything else be scheduled on top of that valuable time. Think of it as "date night" with your business partner.

In business, you don't always have the opportunity to sit down and make sure everything is running smoothly, so succinct, weekly time frames for good old-fashioned face-to-face communication can help work through issues before things grow out of hand. While texting back and forth is good for keeping in touch, getting together once a week in person is a much more robust, meaningful way to communicate.

A Word about Going Into Business with Family (or Close Friends)

Don't assume that family or friends make the best partners in business. In fact, family and friends can be some of the most challenging partnership arrangements. In both instances, it's easy to blur the lines between family/friendship and business.

One of the biggest challenges is ensuring that the family or friend fits the role they are in. It's natural to want to hire Cousin Joe because he needs a job, but if he's bad with numbers he should not be in accounting.

Similarly, don't assume that a friend you hang with is a good fit in business. Even if your dream is to start a microbrewery, your drinking buddy may not be the best person to go into business with—particularly if they have a habit of running up a tab.

In our case, being in business together hasn't always been easy, even though we're family. But we're brothers and we love each other. We want to make sure our business relationship doesn't impact our personal relationship, so we don't let anything become an impasse to moving forward and being successful.

Sometimes it's easy for partners in a start-up to try to do it all. Maybe it's a matter of not wanting to invest in outside help, or not being ready to share the inner workings of the company. Whatever the reason, there comes a point where it's time to look at the value of the company leaders' time. By assigning a dollar amount to that time—$150 to $250 per hour for a CEO—it becomes clearer what roles or functions to hire out. With some parts of the company, it's almost better to outsource, at least until the company reaches the point where it's more effective to bring a function in-house. For instance, if one of the partners is spending five hours a week learning accounting software when those same five hours could be spent bringing in new business, then maybe the company needs to hire an outside accounting firm until it can bring in a chief financial officer.

The primary focus of the business owners should be on building the business by bringing in clients and providing quality service or a quality product. Anything else can be outsourced until the company grows.

The Value of Two—or More

When all is said and done, in spite of the challenges, the partnership can be a very valuable organizational structure. As a couple or a group, by being flexible and organized, you can do much more collectively than as a sole proprietor taking on everything by yourself. If the partners are chosen correctly, the output of the partnership can grow exponentially.

It is nice to have a partner to help share the load. But relationships can be rocky at times. As in a marriage, you have to know your partner, figure out your roles, and understand and work with your strengths and weaknesses.

As for us and our partnership—we're in a great place now, but it took some time to arrive at this point. With the right partner and the right mindset, you can make it work.

Rome Wasn't Built in a Day

Young companies often suffer from "build-it-and-they-will-come" syndrome. They want to start out big in hopes of attracting customers to their business. In fact, we've seen physical therapy practices start out by building a big facility full of fancy equipment thinking they'll fill it with patients. Then, for any number of reasons, the patients don't come and the business closes down.

It's great to dream big. But it's also important to set realistic expectations when starting and then growing a business. That's been one of the keys to the success of Sterling Staffing Solutions. By being realistic about our ability to grow, and then carefully planning, researching, and reassessing as we went, we've gone from having a single person manning a phone from their home to a five-thousand-square-foot headquarters in Sugar Land, Texas, where twenty employees oversee administration for a team of eight hundred contract clinicians in remote offices.

It's great to dream big. But it's also important to set realistic expectations when starting and then growing a business.

To recap some of how we started: We began by researching to ensure we had a niche. Then we put together a business plan that included growing very methodically. We started with one administrative person working out of their home answering the phone while we both continued working in our separate fields—physical therapy and oil and gas. Outside of the electronic medical records system we set up from the start, there were very few expenses. That was 2011.

A year later, with the staffing business growing, that one person working remotely moved to an office at the already established Sterling Physical Therapy and Wellness clinic. That was our first office-based employee. Then the company took off, and in 2013 it moved to the first office of its own, a thousand-square-foot space. Three years later, we outgrew that space and relocated to the five-thousand-square-foot office where we are operating today. Only during that last move did we both step into full-time roles at the staffing company. That's when the company really began to take off.

Today, we have branches in Houston, Dallas/Fort Worth, Austin, and San Antonio, Texas; Oklahoma City and Tulsa, Oklahoma; and Baton Rouge, Louisiana.

When we started expanding the company, we kept the focus of services fairly narrow. Originally, we staffed only for physical therapy, so we were looking only at capturing more of that business—our goal was to capture the entire physical therapy staffing market in our service area.

Then we focused on location. At first, we decided to stay within the greater Houston area. Then we decided to branch into the suburbs of Houston.

After that, we looked at what other specialties we could provide in addition to physical therapy. That led us to staff for other disciplines. We offered occupational therapy and then speech therapy, and then we branched into social work, followed by skilled nursing. Now we're staffing technicians, aides, and even medical doctors.

The PRR Model

We were able to continually add disciplines to our staffing services by employing what we refer to as the PRR model: plan, reassess, repeat. It's a very basic, yet very effective, model for growing or evolving a business.

With the PRR model, you put together a plan—this happens throughout the business life cycle and includes both short- and long-term goals. Then you continually reassess to determine whether you are on track with that plan and readjust as needed, creating a new plan going forward. Reassess your business offerings, the current business landscape, and your operations on a consistent basis. Trends and technology change almost daily, so the market can change almost daily. While you may not face much competition today or even this year, next year could be a completely different ball game. That's why it is crucial to remain nimble and to ensure that the product you're offering is cutting edge and technology driven, and that it provides your consumers with what they really need. Finally, repeat the planning and reassessing with each step of the evolution. Plan, reassess, repeat. Plan, reassess, repeat—that's how to grow steadily and measurably.

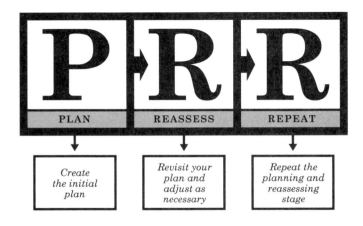

When deciding what cities and states to expand into, the strongest draw for us was areas that had higher concentrations of home health agencies. Since we provide services, specialists, and clinicians to home health patients, we needed to find areas that had those agencies to approach to become our clients. We also knew that home health patients for the most part are elderly or, secondarily, middle-aged. Most have Medicare insurance, which usually means they are sixty-five and older. So, we determined that we needed to find cities and states with a high population of older individuals—a high population of boomers and geriatric people.

When we identified a likely area, we looked at the competition in our niche market and at how far those areas were from where we currently reside. We didn't want to overextend our bandwidth, because we knew that to maintain our growth, we had to effectively manage it.

By considering all these factors, we determined that we could transition into neighboring Oklahoma without a great number of hurdles. We had both attended college there, so we already had a database of clinicians and therapists who had relationships with home health agencies.

Since Louisiana is also a neighbor of Texas, and quite a few of our contractors were actually transplants from that state, we also had numerous relationships there. That made it easier to branch into Baton Rouge. As we write this book, we are researching the viability of expanding into areas as far away as Florida and California.

Our technology-based model has allowed us to remain largely a remote operation. All documentation, medical records, and billing are done online. We communicate largely via text and email. We even conduct interviews for our contractors via the internet using Skype. That interview model works for us because contractors are intensively vetted: each contractor's credentials must be checked (since each has to be licensed by the state in which they operate), their backgrounds must be checked, their inoculations must be up to date, and they must pass a skills checklist.

Planned, researched, measured growth—that's how we have reached our current level of success. That's also how we intend to keep growing. In fact, our story mirrors how multimillion-dollar businesses typically grow. Most large organizations are not instantaneous successes; bursts of growth are not sustainable. Take, for example, these organizations that started small but today are brands known to almost everyone:

Berkshire Hathaway: In the 1960s, Warren Buffett began buying shares of Berkshire Hathaway (approximately $7.50 per share). At the time, the Massachusetts-based cotton mill was producing linings for men's suits. The textile operation itself struggled, but today's Berkshire Hathaway is a multibillion-dollar conglomerate of more than fifty businesses that include commonly known names like Fruit of the Loom, GEICO, and Dairy Queen.[15]

Taco Bell: Glen Bell, the founder of Taco Bell, began his foray into the restaurant business in 1946 with a hot dog stand in San Bernardino, California. He then opened a takeout-only shop and was for years the company's only employee, but tacos didn't appear on the menu until the 1950s.[16] Over time, Bell started and sold numerous businesses, changing the menu, company name and location, and ownership. Then, in 1962, he opened his first Taco Bell, took advantage of the trend in franchising, and the rest is history. In 1978, PepsiCo purchased Taco Bell for nearly $125 million in stock.[17]

Avon: Avon began when salesman David McConnell gave away perfume samples as perks to the stay-at-home women who bought his door-to-door wares. The model of employing women as sales reps came when McConnell recognized the product passion and networking acumen that women had. That was 1886.[18] Today Avon is a company of more than $1.3 billion in annual revenue.[19]

Tiffany & Co.: What was started by Charles Lewis Tiffany as a "stationery and fancy goods" business has grown into a company defined by its dazzling diamonds, unique jewelry designs, other special items, and little blue box.[20] From its 1837 opening-day sales of $4.98, Tiffany & Co. has grown into a company of $4.2 billion in worldwide net sales.[21]

While these are examples of clearly successful organizations, it's been estimated that 25 percent of all businesses fail during their first year in business, and nearly half are gone by the third year.[22] In fact, one study found that fewer than 1.5 percent of businesses consistently added to their employee numbers over a five-year period.[23] Those that managed to do so had one key commonality: slow, steady growth.[24]

The Business Timetable

It takes time to grow into an organization of scale. That means doing the research, creating a plan, putting in the work, and staying the course. That's what makes for a sustainable company.

Companies tend to go through several phases in their journey.[25] The time spent in each phase can vary with industry, region, market demand, and supply availability. If desiring a high growth model, each phase should last no more than two to three years, maximum. The key is to recognize the phase you are in, the challenges therein, and how to quickly overcome those challenges and reach the next phase.

Here is a basic timetable of how most companies evolve over time:

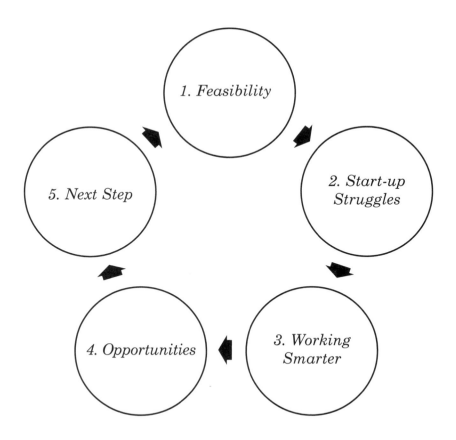

The Feasibility Phase

The first phase, as we discussed in principle one, "Discover Your Niche" is discovering your niche. This phase involves conducting research to vet the idea for the business, putting together the business plan, securing business partners, and identifying banking relationships for capital. For us, the first phase was about recognizing that it made sense to pursue a staffing company, because the clinic was receiving phone calls from therapists trying to find work and from home health agencies looking for therapists. We conducted the research, vetted the idea, built a business plan, and obtained capital to move forward, and then we launched the business.

The Start-Up Struggles Phase

Some painful decisions are made in the start-up phase. It takes a lot of time away from home, financial commitment, and emotional sacrifice to launch a company or idea.

For us, it came down to staying with our main revenue- or compensation-generating positions, and operating Sterling Staffing Solutions as something of a side venture. We had to find one person who could be relied on to work remotely and focus on the staffing business, since neither of us were able to fully commit. But we still put in sixteen-hour days—eight hours at our full-time gigs and then six to eight hours daily trying to launch the staffing company. That required a lot of sacrifice from us and from our families and loved ones. That's why, in this phase, it's important to make sure that those closest to you are committed to the struggle.

It wasn't until we both fully committed and jumped in full time that we started seeing huge growth. But there's a time and a place to make that transition, and for us it meant waiting a few years until we had a well-oiled operation and had conducted our research to know that it was time to grow.

The Working-Smarter Phase

This phase is about preparing to grow. For the staffing company, it meant establishing ourselves as a market leader. We knew that we were better than others in the staffing business. We had established a model and just needed to standardize it so that it could be scaled to work not only in Houston but also in other cities, states, and even countries. In this phase, the company is mentally moving from working hard to working smart, something we will talk more about in principle nine, "Where the Eagles Fly."

The Opportunities Phase

This is the phase many start-ups dream of. In this phase, the business model is vetted, working, and growing consistently, and it can confidently be used to expand the business into other opportunities. Those expansion opportunities may be via acquisition of other companies or by expanding into new products, services, or markets. They may involve forming strategic partnerships with different companies that operate in the same industry or in complementing sectors.

We determine which opportunities to pursue by employing our six o's technique. By taking a deep dive into these six categories, we can make better decisions on moving forward:

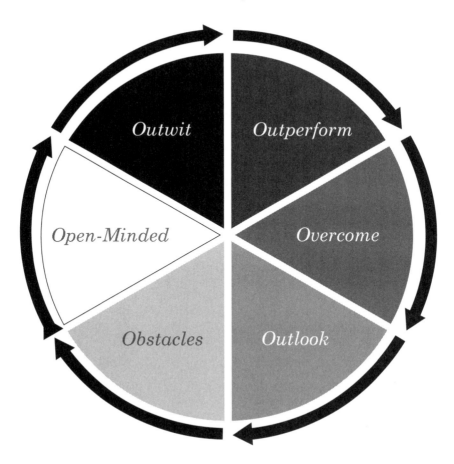

1. **Outperform** regards the things that set an organization apart from the competition. Where does the team excel? Is it quality products and services, loyal customers, a unique use of technology? If you make widgets, what makes those widgets the best in the business?

2. **Overcome** regards areas that need improvement. What is keeping the company from being competitive? Does it have too much employee turnover? Is its supply chain unreliable? Is it weighed down by too much debt or held back by lack of capital? If your widgets are made of imported steel, what happens when trade relations change?

3. **Outlook** regards looking at current trends, market or industry changes, evolving customer demographics, environmental or political factors, or even new training or talent. If your widgets are the best in the business but only supply one industry, what other industries also need widgets?

4. **Obstacles** are factors that have the potential to inflict harm. Common obstacles for most organizations include rising expenses and increased competition. What will happen if a new widget maker moves in and cuts your business in half? Are you ready to diversify? How can your organization's capabilities—its tools and skill sets—create a widget or other component for another industry?

5. **Open-mindedness** regards how you approach your staff, clients, and business coach when developing a plan. It's about having open meetings with staff and facilitating a

group thinking process to ensure that the plan that is being formulated has everyone's buy-in. It's also about talking with clients and trying to find out their pain points, then making sure that every issue is addressed. It's even observing competitors and everything else that is happening in the industry to avoid ending up in a situation where an "Amazon" comes in and takes away business because they're smarter, more efficient, and more technically minded.

6. **Outwit** regards the goal of the plan you will create using the first five o's. The plan should be smart, well thought out, and relevant to your organization.

In performing a six o's deep dive, look at the categories from internal and external points of view: What strengths, weaknesses, opportunities, and threats exist within the organization and from outside factors? Look at how opportunities and threats from external factors relate to strengths and weaknesses on the inside to help determine whether an objective is attainable and to create a strategy to move forward. Also consider personal and professional perspectives.

Ideally, bring together the entire team when performing a six o's deep dive, because the marketing group, clinical team, and recruiters will all have different insights.

Brainstorm by simply throwing out ideas. Remember, no idea is a bad idea. When we do our six o's deep dive, we use our whiteboard and sticky notes, since sometimes an idea may fit a couple of categories, or an idea may appear to fit one category but then, as more ideas surface, move to a different one.

Boil every category down to five main points. What five ways do you outperform competitors? What five areas need to be improved before operations are shut down? What five trends are relevant to your organization? What five obstacles must be overcome? If you fall short of five in one category, look to another for ideas. For instance, if you are short of five areas where the company outperforms, look at the outlook category to see whether the company is in itself a trend-setter. Also focus on the areas that need improvement—these are what keep your bucket from being full (remember the goal-setting discussion in principle two, "Is There Any 'There' There?").

The six o's are such an important tool that it can be used anytime. And it's not something that should be rushed—we have even devoted several days to using the tool in planning. That allows us to flesh out the ideas in great detail, which may require research or data mining. For instance, if an area of needed improvement is revealed during the brainstorming session, it may mean digging into some data or tracking some results to understand where the issue lies. If a viable trend involves deploying new technology, new turf left in the wake of another organization's departure, or the potential to merge with another organization, then research will reveal whether a viable outlook truly exists.

Once you've completed your six o's, actionable steps must be developed for all the components of each category and used as part of goal setting.

The Next-Step Phase

This phase involves looking at the future of the company under new leadership. It may mean formulating an exit strategy for the founders or guiding leaders, or deciding whether to take the company public, or looking into selling the company or passing it on to another generation.

Growth doesn't happen without obstacles that have to be overcome. Indeed, there will be moments and days of doubt throughout the journey of leading and growing a business. But with some planning and good decision making, you can grow and build a venture through the five phases.

Let's look at some of the challenges and triggers of that can occur during growth.

Growing Pains—and Wins

We have a policy of letting our home health agency customers know within two hours whether we have the staff to serve their patient. That policy also states that we will complete an evaluation of the patient within forty-eight hours, meaning that the therapist will visit the patient within forty-eight hours of receiving the referral from the home health agency. We also guarantee to minimize the number of missed visits with each patient—if the patient is scheduled for three visits per week, then they will have three visits per week, even if that means the therapist must work on Saturday. Those are the kinds of guarantees that have made us the top staffing company.

Those policies worked great until one month when we ended up with twice as many referrals as we were accustomed to. Not only did we not meet our guarantee, but we also lost some major home health agency contracts. The agencies had given us the opportunity to see their patients, we told them we could do the work, and then we weren't able to. That caused them to pull all their business.

That was a point at which we were unable to manage or sustain our growth. The cost? Thousands of dollars in contracts and a ding on our reputation. Fortunately, we were able to come up with a reconciliation plan that let us rebound, and today we have those contracts and more.

Growing too fast and not being prepared for that growth can have disastrous results for a company, causing a loss of revenue, a marred reputation, or, worse, shuttering the doors. Planning for growth is about more than just the valleys, when business is super slow and expenses still have to be paid. It also means planning for the peaks, when the company doesn't have the capacity to support its workload. Either of these can lead to trouble.

A number of factors can trigger or inhibit growth. Here are a few that may affect the journey. Be aware of these to avoid pitfalls and recognize opportunities.

All Revenue Is Not Good Revenue

Determine caps for the company's gross profit and operating margins to help define which opportunities are worth pursuing. In our efforts to expand, we found a number of opportunities that would give us a significant amount of additional revenue but would not generate a comfortable profit margin, so we passed on them.

Consider the Risk

If the business model is unfamiliar to you, how much is involved in taking on an entirely new type of venture? Even though health care is a very regulated industry, as the staffing company, we're the middleman. A lot of the regulatory responsibilities pertaining to Medicare and Medicaid are on the home health agencies. That allows us to be somewhat free of the scrutiny of government regulation, since our revenue comes from the home health agencies, not directly from Medicare or Medicaid. When considering opportunities outside our current niche, we passed on some business models that we considered too risky.

Have Realistic Expectations

Growth percentages can be very high in the start-up years. For instance, if you make $50,000 in your first year of revenue and then jump to $500,000 the next year, that's a 1,000 percent increase in revenue. More realistically, one five-year study found that start-ups grew an average 35 percent annually in their first few years.[26] But that kind of growth is difficult to sustain over the long-term. Growth depends on any number of factors, but generally 10 to 20 percent may be more realistic year over year over the long-term.

Be Ready for Trial and Error

A company may grow because it is super busy, but if its expenses are out of control, it can still go out of business. That can actually happen from having too many customers—how many customers can the company work with and still provide a quality product or service? It's a matter of finding the right balance of customers, staff, and product offerings. Even with extensive planning, it can take a number of tries to develop a business model that is streamlined, scalable, and profitable.

Once the model is developed and working, it's much easier to duplicate in another location. Put the model in writing—the processes, the policies, the number of employees, their roles—all the details in a step-by-step format. That makes it easier to replicate somewhere else.

Look at Walmart, for example. The hub or headquarters is in Bentonville, Arkansas. All the other Walmart stores sell the products and services, but the back-end pieces of the business—the real estate, human resources, payroll, purchasing—are all conducted at the headquarters.

Our model is similar. From our base in Sugar Land—where we have the administrative support—we operate several satellite offices of clinical staff. That allows us to have fairly fixed primary expenses and little in the way of expansion expense.

There are a lot of business software programs available that have templates for different types of businesses. These ideas and plans have already been vetted; they are ideal starting points for anyone considering turning an idea into a company, because they are plans of businesses that have worked in the past.

Mind the Money

Lack of financing can limit growth. Start-ups grow by pursuing and landing contracts, sometimes landing big contracts a little outside their realm. And then comes the matter of resources: Can the company really afford the big contract it just landed that will take it to the next level? Sometimes that means pursuing financing from another source, and if that source is a loan through the Small Business Administration or a financial institution, then a good credit history and a strong business plan will be required.

Using investors is a great way of producing operating revenue. Many successful people are looking for great business ideas and models to invest in. There is even a reality television show, *Shark Tank*, where investors vet business ideas and then fund those deemed worth the risk.

One way to manage funding in a business is with a revolving line of credit; it's there if needed, and it's a good safety net if not needed. That's a good solution for us. If we know that we are growing significantly, we make sure our line of credit is able to cover payroll until we obtain the funds due from the home health agencies that we contract with.

Saving is important as a business just as it is as an individual. Even businesses need a rainy-day fund. Once the business gets going, don't forget to put a little aside.

The money in a business must be constantly monitored. Approaching the financial aspects of the business proactively rather than reactively can keep the doors open.

Focus On Your Core

Even corporate giants can struggle with diversification. Take Northrop Grumman, for instance. Although one of the top defense contractors in the world, the company made an expensive error when attempting to move into the shipbuilding space. In 2001, the aerospace and defense technology behemoth decided to try its hand at shipbuilding for the US Navy. Ten years later, the company ditched the business because the division was simply not in sync with the company's other businesses, and too-thin profit margins were a major drag on the bottom line.[27]

Stay Innovative

A lack of vision can kill a company, particularly in the technology or dot-com world. That nearly happened with Zynga, a video gaming company that rocketed as a start-up but then struggled to maintain its lead. It started with a couple of real wins, Zynga Poker and Mafia Wars, that were downloadable apps. The company made amazing money in the beginning, so it invested millions in data centers to be ahead of its growth. Then it failed to innovate and was slow to recognize when the public started to lose interest in its core products. Ultimately, the company laid off thousands of workers and closed down the data centers it had spent millions to construct. After restructuring, the company is now a powerhouse in the gaming industry, but it's a place that came with some serious hard knocks.[28]

Time Growth

Sometimes success is a matter of being in the right place at the right time. Even corporate giants like Sony know that pain.

Pretty much everyone knows the iPod personal music player was created by Apple, but not everyone realizes that the iPod represents a huge missed opportunity for the electronics technology titan Sony. By the time the iPod came along, Sony was already the portable music industry leader, producing everything from radios to the Walkman. But when Sony came out with its version of what would become the iPod, the technology was expensive and the device didn't hold enough data. There were also concerns with piracy of the content the company owned through its Sony Music division.[29] When the ultra-cool iPod launched, it was smaller, held more tunes, and didn't have the piracy worries, since it didn't own the content.[30] The latter of these issues, some industry experts say, is what really led to Sony missing out on the portable music opportunity—too many working silos led to lack of cooperation across the company's various divisions.

Gain Local Loyalty

When expanding globally, never assume that the area you're stepping into will automatically allow replication of the model. Even in today's connected and virtual world, some areas are not as welcoming to companies that are not perceived to have a local presence. In those instances, setting up a local office in some shape or form may be a necessary early measure to get a foot in the door with customers in the area. That may be as simple as obtaining a local phone number and post office box, or it may mean setting up a physical location.

Customize Compensation Rates

Obviously, compensation rates will vary across international boundaries. But they also vary across the United States and even city to city. For instance, the cost of living in Houston, where we are based, is different than in New York City. The same goes for rates of service—therapy rates across the United States and around the world vary.

Tailor Operational Requirements

While the idea in creating a working business model is to be able to plug it in anywhere you want to operate, the reality is that business requirements can also vary from place to place. For instance, some areas, like Houston, are rife with Medicare and Medicaid fraud. For that reason, there are a lot of checks and balances used in the Houston market that are actually higher standards of quality, but these are perceived differently in other areas. When we began operating in other areas, we found that these higher standards not only were not required, but they were actually offensive to some people.

One such standard was the practice of requiring clinicians to obtain a signature from the patient when they visited his or her home. In fact, the electronics software system we use for record keeping has a built-in global positioning system (GPS), which allows us to capture the patient's electronic signature along with the physical location where the signature was taken. That prevents a signature from being forged without a visit taking place, and ensures that the clinician keeps records current instead of waiting until day's end.

However, while this practice works in areas of heavy fraud, we found that in some areas clinicians perceived the technology as questioning their ethics.

"I'm a therapist, I would never put my license on the line," was a comment we heard more than once. That was a learning experience for us and represents how culture is something to consider when venturing outside your own area.

Promoting Employees

Successful companies have a handful of employees who perform at a higher level than other employees. In some cases, these stellar staff members are ten times more productive than others on the team.[31] The company has identified these stars and knows how to leverage their talent to drive other members of the team. Some managers believe that the only way to keep high performers happy is to promote them into leadership roles. That approach may not be the best option for the employee or the company. Everyone has heard of a star performer being promoted into a key position where they failed miserably. You don't want that to happen. Before you promote a star employee to a management position, make sure the employee is ready for it, and ensure that your team can maintain its quality of work when the employee is gone. Consider alternatives to promotions like:

- lateral moves—Changes in responsibility and/or role can be just as appealing and satisfying as a promotion.

- lateral leaps—In most cases, star performers have the ability to succeed in almost any role. For example, consider moving your star HR professional to a business development role.

➡ focus on skills growth—Improving an employee's skills can significantly boost their morale. At the same time, you could be grooming that person for the next opportunity.

➡ periodic bonuses—Financial incentives go a long way in showing appreciation. It is a small investment in keeping your employees happy.

➡ ad hoc projects—Tap into the employee's passion to fix problems. Assign them a project that will improve your service delivery.[32]

The key is to resist the temptation to promote these high performers and instead maintain them in positions where they continue to contribute to the good of the whole—that's where they are the most productive.

Find Partners to Propel Growth

It can be difficult to maintain growth energy over time. By forging strategic partnerships, however, growth can even speed up. That's exactly what happened when Google's Android was gaining stature in the cell phone market and the company teamed with Samsung.[33] Today the pairing dominates the smartphone world.

Keep It Together

Remember that growth is a great thing—unless it causes unwelcome compromise. For instance, if growing too big too fast causes the company to compromise on quality, then it may be time to scale back and rethink. The best-selling book *The ONE Thing: The Surprisingly Simple Truth Behind Extraordinary Results*, by Gary Keller and Jay Papasan, is a great resource for staying focused and not stretching the company too thin during growth. The wisdom in that volume has helped us stay in line with our core business model and not venture too far outside of what we do in unfamiliar and harmful territory.

Make a plan, be organized, and always put your most professional foot forward. That can keep the company presentable as it scales and expands into uncharted areas.

There will be moments and days of doubt as you grow and build your business, but keep your eye on the prize and you can overcome the obstacles and keep moving forward.

There will be moments and days of doubt as you grow and build your business, but keep your eye on the prize and you can overcome the obstacles and keep moving forward. It also helps to have your team on board, and that comes from selling your idea to your stakeholders.

IMPLEMENTATION

Sell Your Vision

Y ou've vetted your idea, conducted the research, created a plan. You know what your competitors do and don't do well. You know the problem you're trying to solve and how you're going to solve it. Now it's time to speak passionately about what you're doing, about the difference that you bring to the table.

In principle one, "Discover Your Niche" we discussed having a formalized mission and vision as the guiding beacons for how the company operates. The mission and vision statements must be deliberate and lived, and include every stakeholder—the owners, leaders, employees, and customers. The company must have a belief system in place, a culture that makes people want to come to work and give their best work every day.

Once formulated, the vision must be sold internally and externally. Selling the vision of the business can build loyalty with everyone from customers to suppliers to the team working for the company.

One of the biggest challenges for a company leader is to sell their idea and earn the buy-in of the team. All those big ideas mean nothing unless they are communicated effectively and generate excitement across the organization. The goal is to create an engaged team that is motivated to move those ideas forward.

Admittedly, the idea of selling anything can be very intimidating to leaders who are more accustomed to sitting behind a desk and monitoring numbers. But no one can tell the company story better. When you believe passionately in the company's vision, that will come through as you're out there telling the world about your organization. Communicate that vision in the same way that you would tell a story to a family member or a friend. Tell it as if you're trying to convince someone of your conviction—because in essence, you are.

Build a Team of "Salespeople"

For more traction when telling your story, build a team of ambassadors for the company. The goal is for every person in the organization to be a salesperson—not just the marketing, business development, or sales team. Whether they work inside the office every day or they're representing the company in the field, every person in the organization must feel that they are the face of the company to the public. Every day that they're talking to clients, potential clients, and stakeholders, they must be able to sell the vision. They must believe in it so strongly, and understand what the company does so well, that they can sell to others in a very authentic and passionate way.

By investing in employees, you are investing in the business—they will pay it forward by being much more committed to the vision. The goal is to keep them long term, because losing an employee can be a setback to forward progression. It means starting all over again—finding someone who fits in the culture and then undergoing the expense and time of training them. That can be especially challenging in an organization structured with many remote offices (as our company is).

By investing in employees, you are investing in the business—they will pay it forward by being much more committed to the vision.

Build loyalty within by finding out what motivates employees, what makes them want to come to work every day and make a difference. Provide good benefits, including training and education. Also, these days some sort of community outreach or volunteer program goes a long way toward building loyalty. Taking an interest in employees' needs and wants makes it easier for them to sell the vision. When they want to come to work, talking about work in a positive light comes from a place of authenticity.

Today, we operate on a rewards-based system. Our mantra, "If we grow, you grow," has helped staff members become excited about the growth of the business. Using KPIs to measure the success of the business, we're able to offer a quarterly bonus program based on how well the business performs. If we have a successful quarter, then everyone in the company gets a bonus. Offering commission- or incentive-based pay also allows for lower base salaries, then pays employees more based on their performance—not for just showing up and working eight to five. Such incentives give employees a little something extra to strive for. If staff members are expected to excel, an incentive can give them a reason to show up day after day and even come together toward a common goal, which is to make the business succeed.

One way to make the vision relatable for every member of the team is to have each staff member define what the vision means to them. That can make the vision more personal to them, something they can feel comfortable believing and supporting.

It's also easier to build loyalty by hiring people who have already begun to buy into the vision. During the interview process, look for what motivates a candidate to do well in their role.

- Generation Z individuals are motivated by skills training, mentoring relationships, continuous feedback, and the company culture. They tend to value recognition, time off, and flexible schedules.

- Millennials are motivated by working for a company that respects them, aligns with their values, and appreciates their contributions to the company.

- Gen Xers are motivated by growth opportunities, autonomy to make decisions, and avenues to be a mentee and a mentor.

- Baby boomers are motivated by promotions, professional development, a desire to be in a position of authority, and having their expertise valued and acknowledged.

Understanding what motivates the employee candidate can help address the job offer in a way that makes sense to them and encourages them to join your team.

In addition to the internal team, the vision must also be sold to customers and other stakeholders outside the company.

Selling the Vision to Customers

It takes a certain type of personality to be in sales. Although some leaders are more comfortable in other areas of the business—the last thing they want to do is sell—they often have more opportunities to meet with a prospect than do members of the sales and marketing team.

We have found that potential clients value the owner or a key leader of the company taking the time to see them personally. It shows that we're very serious about doing business with them. Obviously, there may come a point where the leader may not be able to make those face-to-face sales calls, but many customers enjoy having a relationship that allows them to pick up the phone and talk with a key leader when a situation calls for it. They like knowing that they're working with the person calling the shots in the business, and that they also have someone to hold accountable if something goes wrong.

However, a sales or marketing professional can in some ways serve as a buffer between top decision makers and customers, helping to reduce those instances where the leader has to be involved in bringing a new client on board or making a deal. This can actually allow the company to stand firmer in its pricing and processes. When a sales professional has to run a special pricing request up the ladder to management, sometimes the reply can be a "no." That "no" is not as easy to produce when the decision maker is face-to-face with a customer and there's a sense of obligation to make the customer happy.

At some point, there may be a need to hire a team member whose specific role is to be the public face as a sales, marketing, or business development professional, and you will need to find the right talent to deliver the right message. When we made the decision to bring on a high-level business development executive, the candidate we hired really exploded our business and took us to the next level.

When hiring sales and marketing professionals, look for people with experience and, ideally, with contacts in your industry. Ethics are also important—you don't want someone trying to sell something they don't believe in. They must have the integrity to sell what the company can deliver, but also not want to put their own integrity on the line by working for a company that doesn't deliver as promised. They must be able to hold the internal team accountable, and work with the team to ensure that everyone is happy—from the customer to the company.

Selling the vision to clients is about understanding their issues. Using open-ended questions can help uncover the issues they have had in the past, then allow you to customize a response with information that addresses their specific needs without overwhelming them with too much information that they don't value.

In our industry, many clients want to know that the service is high quality, but they're also focused on the bottom line—a common issue in many industries. But selling on price can be a dangerous place to do business—it means compromising, sometimes to the detriment of the company.

When selling on price, approach it from the perspective of how much the customer will save by using your better-quality service. In some industries, that may boil down to the cost of avoiding risk—make the case to the customer that cheaper isn't always better and can even place them in a compromising situation. For instance, as a staffing agency, it's critical for our customers to know that their patients are well cared for. Using a reputable company is crucial, even if it costs a little more.

Make a Lasting Impression

Selling the vision externally is largely accomplished through marketing, sales, business development, and advertising—these are essential in a start-up. Creating a brand gives the company an identity that separates it in a saturated or highly competitive market.

Most potential customers see a company's marketing materials before the initial contact. Having a professional look with quality marketing collateral can make the right first impression. Whether it's a flyer in the mail, an email campaign, a social media advertisement, a website, or a review on Yelp, it's critically important to present a quality brand. That brand can do some of the work for you in building loyalty from customers and the general public.

Depending on the industry and the message being conveyed, the branding may have a very professional look or appear more casual, conservative, or even playful. For instance, a pediatric dentistry office will likely want branding that shows children enjoying their experience to help remove the fear of a visit to the dentist for young patients. And, obviously, the branding will be vastly different for a supermarket and a mobile car wash and a law office.

Whatever the brand, it must create a perception about the company very quickly and concisely. Its goal is to create brand advocates, customers who look to your company first to fill their needs for the product or service you sell. They must be inspired to initiate the first phone call to begin a conversation that leads to a long-term customer relationship.

Remember, authenticity and transparency are key in all forms of marketing. Match your message to the client's needs and wants, and you'll win the business. Also remember that every form of marketing should state the reasons the customer should do business with your company, and always end with a call to action: "Call us today"; "Send this in today"; "Sign here and we'll start right away." That sense of urgency is often what it takes for people to pull the trigger and say yes to doing business with you.

There are different tools to help put that brand together and deliver the most return for your marketing dollar. Here are some of the tools we use:

Word-of-Mouth Marketing (WOMM)

One of the most powerful tools costs nothing and can net the most return. Word-of-mouth marketing starts with leaders and ambassadors telling the company's story, then branches out from the good relationships built with customers. According to Nielsen, the global measurement and data analytics company, 83 percent of consumers worldwide trust recommendations from family and friends over advertising, and 66 percent said they trust online consumer opinions.[34] So the more your story is told in a positive light, the more it grows simply by word of mouth.

Social Media

The power of social media cannot be overstated. Nearly everyone is connected online in some form or manner. Despite its inconsistencies and pitfalls, social media is one of the most trusted forms of advertising.[35]

A survey of more than two thousand people ages eighteen and over found that more than half (56 percent) follow brands on social media to learn more about their products. Respondents to the survey said they use social networks to browse for items and that images found on those sites influenced their purchases.[36]

Success in using social media relies on several factors:

POSTING REGULARLY

Timeliness is key with social media. Social media and messaging accounts for approximately one of every three minutes that users are on the internet.[37]

MAKING RELEVANT POSTINGS

Your efforts will have more traction if the message is relevant to the audience. That means you must know who your target audience is, what they need, and which form of communication speaks to them. For instance, in the health care industry, communicating with patients in a manner that speaks to them is vastly different than what's needed to gain the attention of a physician. Word choice alone can make that difference—for example, while a physician's ears may perk up at "myocardial infarction," a patient's eyes may gloss over at the term. (Use the words "heart attack" and patients will hear the message loud and clear.)

USING PHOTOS AND VIDEOS

The adage "a picture is worth a thousand words" has become more relevant than ever thanks to sites like Instagram, which has grown from one million active monthly users after its launch in 2010 to more than eight hundred million active users.[38] Instagram is an amazing tool for showing before-and-after results or testimonials from smiling, happy clients. Online sites like YouTube are also excellent for telling your story in video format. Even a simple video made with a smartphone can go a long way with consumers.

CREATING CAMPAIGNS

There are management tools that allow you to post across all of your social media channels at the same time. These can be very effective in managing a social media campaign, which is a coordinated effort to increase focus, target traffic, and measure the results of a message shared online.

ENGAGING YOUR AUDIENCE

Play games with the audience to promote interaction. Offer deals, discounts, swag, and other giveaways as rewards for participation and for winning.

BEING RESPONSIVE

Social media users want information, and they want it now. While the average user will wait four hours for a brand to respond to a posting, the average response time for most brands is ten hours. [39] Some networks even note your level of responsiveness, letting customers know that your company answers in a timely manner and even estimating your response time.[40]

Social media can be a super powerful tool, but it can also cause some real harm. Reviews, especially, can be a friend or a foe. And it doesn't matter how many great experiences a company has, it only takes one negative review to cause a lot of grief.

To combat negative online reviews, build up a database of good reviews by asking satisfied clients to comment online. Many companies offer an incentive such as a discount on future purchases once a review is complete. Even tagging the company online when posting photos to Facebook or other pages can have a positive impact, personalizing the company and making it more relatable.

Perhaps the best way to combat negative reviews is to be responsive and even use the review as an opportunity to engage. Admit to the mistake, apologize, tout positive aspects of the company, and potentially even offer reparations. These measures can go a long way toward silencing critics. According to Shama Hyder, author of *The Zen of Social Media Marketing*, "People are not looking for perfection online. What they're really looking for is humanity and a genuine response, so a negative review can be a great opportunity to respond in a positive and transparent manner. And that has a good impact on all your customers."[41]

A Strong, Up-to-Date Online Presence

Your online presence should include an up-to-date website (your company's virtual front door), an established Yelp page, and an established Google Plus page or Google page. With those three sites, your online presence is golden.

Investing in search engine optimization (SEO) is a plus when using the internet to tell your story. SEO can help you have a direct marketing campaign online that targets consumers for your product or service. Using SEO can help improve your rankings and drive traffic to your online presence.

Print Media

Print can be one of the costlier parts of marketing, and your need for it may depend on your industry, product, and target audience. Print media may include anything from direct mail pieces that reach the mailboxes of potential consumers, to brochures and handouts used in-office or at trade shows and events, to advertisements in magazines or journals. To get the most for your print marketing dollar, be sure to track your return on investment (ROI) efforts with coupons, special discount codes, or a simple "How did you hear about us?" inquiry with each call that comes into your company.

Cold Calling

Perhaps the most expensive type of marketing is the cost of paying a representative for cold-calling consumers. In addition to your rep's salary, you're paying for their training, travel, and any materials they need to market the company. Depending on your situation, this may be the best option or it may be the one that gives you the least bang for your buck.

Extra Efforts Gain Legitimacy

When we opened our doors, we discovered very early on that our marketing was narrowly focused—we marketed to home health agencies, but few outside the industry were aware of us. We knew we needed to legitimize our brand and decided that one way to do that would be to win awards. We thought that those wins would put our name on a bigger stage and potentially open us up for other opportunities with new clients and clinicians.

In our efforts, we found that we were actually quite competitive, netting the top prize in a number of awards. We hired a public relations person to help us promote the awards, which gave us exposure to a larger audience. Over time, the awards helped build our reputation and increased loyalty from our current staffing companies.

A good reputation can be a big plus in strengthening the brand and having the public hold the company in a higher regard. Clients, customers, and the community as a whole are inclined to be more forgiving if an award-winning company errs in judgment at some point. When a company has won awards for being the best at something, a rare misstep has a better chance of being viewed as a hiccup.

Community outreach can also help build a good reputation. Employees especially are motivated by being a part of a company that has a bigger vision to make a difference, not just make profits. When people see your brand doing good in the community, they'll want to be part of that effort—this includes employees and others in the community. After all, most people enter the health care industry because they genuinely want to make a difference—they want to improve the health or lives of the patients they see. When they are backed by a company that supports those desires, they are empowered to make a positive impact every working day.

Lead with the CARES Model

After Hurricane Harvey hit Houston, our staff came together to participate in Habitat for Humanity to help the people who were flooded out. We went into homes together and helped remove wet drywall, carpet, and other moldy and mildewed items so that the remodelers could come in and do their jobs.

Going the extra mile is a common trait among the clinicians we staff, stemming from their desire to ensure quality care for every patient they see. For those patients with social or economic hardships that go beyond home health, the clinicians often take it upon themselves to identify those extra needs and find other ways to ensure that the patient receives the assistance they need.

What these clinicians are doing is reflected in our model for how we interact with our stakeholders, which we call the CARES model. As the name implies, the CARES model is focused on caring for our stakeholders, both internal and external. Here's how we break it down:

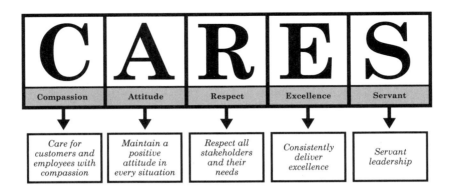

Compassion

It's about caring for the needs of all stakeholders with the same sense of compassion.

Two companies that practice the "C" in CARES for their stake-holder employees are Facebook and Google. For its North American employees, Facebook offers enviable perks such as three weeks of paid vacation for full-time employees, paid time off and $4,000 in cash for new parents, financial aid for adoption fees, a wellness allowance for gym memberships or activities geared toward healthy activities, on-site extras for Menlo Park employees that include free meals and snacks, a barber shop, health and dental care services, an arcade, valet parking, and a free electric car charging station.[42]

Google, meanwhile, literally takes care of its people from cradle to grave. New parents receive time off during which bonuses are still awarded and stock continues to vest, and there is an on-site daycare for kids. Development is encouraged through ongoing learning and career advances. On-site extras also include free gourmet food and drinks, pets brought from home, fitness classes, internal tech support, and opportunities to earn credit toward massages. And creativity is fostered by extended time-off allowances and an 80/20 policy that permits employees to spend 80 percent of their time on company projects and 20 percent pursuing a passion that may benefit Google.[43]

But Ritz-Carlton may wear the crown for the "C" in CARES with its compassion toward its customers. At one of the Ritz-Carlton Hotels, a guest made a request for the recovery of his young son's beloved bed toy, a stuffed giraffe by the name of Joshie. When Joshie came up missing and was retrieved in the hotel laundry, the father requested that the staff take a photo of the giraffe next to the pool to validate his story to his son that the lost toy had simply stayed behind to extend its vacation. The staff not only recovered and returned the toy to the young boy, but also sent along a box of Ritz-Carlton swag and a photo album of the giraffe enjoying its vacation poolside, getting a massage, making new friends with other real and stuffed "critters," and more.[44]

Attitude

Even more important than offering perks is creating a positive work environment, one that fosters a positive attitude with every interaction. Even on a phone call, a smile can make all the difference, bringing a positive tone to the conversation. In fact, one study found that a positive workplace is more effective and productive.[45] According to the study, positive practices improve emotions and amplify creativity;

provide a buffer for negativity, making it easier to handle challenges; and improve a company's ability to attract employees and gain their loyalty.[46]

Southwest Airlines understands the value of creating a positive work environment to excite its employees about their jobs. Customers point to the airline's friendly, helpful employees as the reason for their loyalty. That happens because employees feel as if they are part of a team, and they are empowered to make decisions to keep customers happy.[47]

Respect

This piece of the CARES model is especially important to us. Our therapists see many geriatric patients who are homebound, but just because they are home most of the time does not mean appointment times can be lax. Patients' schedules and private time are important to them and must be respected. That means calling ahead to schedule an appointment, confirming the appointment beforehand, and then showing up at the scheduled time or giving a courtesy call if running late.

Earning the respect of customers is something that REI, the outdoor clothing and gear company, has mastered. How? By first showing its customers and its employees respect. In a bold move, on Black Friday 2015 (and every year since), stores remained closed while the company encouraged employees and customers to spend time outdoors with family and friends. The payoff? An increase in revenue of 9.3 percent (to $2.4 billion), a 23 percent increase in digital sales for the year.[48]

Excellence

This piece of the CARES model encompasses every aspect of operations. We want to always be great in everything we do. We want our reputation to be one in which people expect excellence of the organization.

Boeing is one company that has truly embedded innovation and excellence within its culture, and the results have been staggering. In 1998, it took Boeing 71 days to assemble its 777 aircraft—today it takes just 37. By introducing a grass roots culture of innovation and excellence, the aerospace giant also managed to shave an incredible nine days off the final assembly of its 737, going from 20 days to 11.[49]

Servant Leadership

Operating from a servant leadership perspective means serving everyone—from employees, to customers and vendors, to the community.

In the wake of Hurricane Harvey, a Houston-based chain, Gallery Furniture, opened two of its stores to displaced residents. The stores provided residents in need of shelter—and their pets—with beds, food, and restrooms.[50]

Identifying Our Stakeholders

In formulating the CARES model, we started by identifying all of the stakeholders affected by our business. We wanted to address each stakeholder in a way that let them know that we care and that we are there to help them succeed.

Every business has at least three major stakeholders: (1) the customer or client that is purchasing or receiving the product or service, (2) the vendors or providers that supply the product or service being sold, and (3) the employees who must be on board with the company's mission and vision. Here's how we define these three types of stakeholders:

1. **Customers/clients.** For us, the customers are health care agencies. We also consider the patient of the home health agency to be our customer, so we focus on being more of a care partner with each home health agency. We want them to know that we're working with them to ensure their company is a success. For other health care providers, patients themselves may be the customers.

2. **Vendors.** In the commercial space, these are the suppliers that provide materials or products. In our space, vendors are the providers of care—the clinicians and therapists.

3. **Employees.** Since we believe so strongly that employees are stakeholders, we invest heavily in ensuring that they feel they are part of the team.

In the health care space, identifying the various stakeholders can be a bit complex, because there are many additional layers. For instance, we contract with home health agencies, and they contract with payers such as Blue Cross Blue Shield, Aetna, United, Medicare, Medicaid, or other insurers. They are reimbursed from those entities for the care that they manage, and they subcontract our company to provide that care. Therefore, the work that our clinicians do must meet the quality standards and regulatory requirements administratively for Medicare, Medicaid, and all the other payers.

When considering the stakeholders in any business, look all the way upstream and downstream to determine whom the company touches. Depending on the industry and product or service being provided, the stakeholders may be your customers or your customer's customers.

Stakeholders may also include banks or investors—creditors that have a vested interest in the company's success. Government or regulatory bodies, any entity that the company reports to such as a board of directors, or any entity that oversees rules and regulations that the company must abide by are also stakeholders. In our case, those include the regulators that oversee the licensing for the therapists that we employ as contractors.

We also view the company itself as a stakeholder, because at the end of the day we must also look out for its interests. We must ensure that we're caring for the company and that it's growing in a feasible and healthy manner so that it can take care of all the stakeholders.

Once the stakeholders are identified, their needs must be understood, communicated across the business, and addressed with the CARES model.

Delivering CARES

Communication is one key to delivering the CARES model, but that can be a challenge in many industries, particularly in those that operate in antiquated business models. That's the case with health care. Many health care providers are still, surprisingly, very paper based, using faxes for referrals instead of relying on an electronic medical records system. However, many others on the inside in this industry don't see the current health care model as broken. They don't even view health care as a business. But health care is a business just like any other, and as with any business, there are certain aspects to be considered: Who is the competition? What differentiates the business? How can technology put us ahead of the curve?

The dental industry seems to understand the importance of innovation. It used to be that people only sought out dentistry when they had a problem—much like current medicine. But in the last few decades, the dental industry as a whole has redefined itself. Today it's commonplace for people to have regular checkups every year to ensure the health of their teeth and gums and to place themselves ahead of any problems. Technology has also changed the dental industry. Take Invisalign, for instance, which has revolutionized orthodontics. For years, straightening teeth was done primarily with brackets and wires. Then someone took it to a new level with plastic aligners that are custom fitted to the teeth.

Obviously, when it comes to technology, health care excels. There are many innovations in health care from a clinical perspective. Heavy investment in ongoing research and development has delivered incredible advances that are saving lives. In the rehabilitation space alone, there are amazing advances that are literally putting people back on their feet—some of these advances are light years away from where rehab was only a few decades ago.

Where the disconnect in health care occurs is on the administrative side. That's where innovation and the use of technology is lacking.

But that's not the case with our organization. We use technology to ensure that communication across the organization is fast and effective and makes us more accessible to our clients, staff, and other stakeholders. We still fax if it benefits our clients, but as often as possible we use electronic referrals, or e-referrals. An e-referral converts a faxed document into an email, which is then sent to staff, doctors, and home health agencies. Once it's in email form, it can stay in that form for all future communication.

We also use texting for a good portion of our communication, using text campaigns to reach our contractors in real time. This helps us convey needed information without having to send them an email that they may not retrieve as quickly or interrupt them with a phone call when they are busy working with a patient. Of course, we also use phone and email for communication, but texting is often faster and more efficient for our needs. We are also very big on using instant messaging, also known as chat, even across the office. This technology actually improves productivity by allowing for conversation with less interruption of workflow—chatting minimizes the number of less efficient face-to-face meetings by providing a means for quick question-and-answer sessions.

Whatever form it takes, communication via technology helps ensure that we don't miss vital information. It helps us turn a one-way expression of needs into a two-way interaction that delivers on our CARES model.

Communication also makes us an organization that is nimbler and in sync. By communicating constantly and effectively, we can make changes far more rapidly. By being connected and attuned to the CARES model as a team, we consistently make a difference in people's lives.

That difference is evident in the extras, like on-call administrative staff on weekends—a service unheard of in health care. On-call helps provide coverage outside typical business hours, allowing needs to be met without having to wait until Monday. Staff also consistently work through lunch—it's hard to turn them off, because they're so concerned about taking care of clients and making sure nothing is left undone. They are also versed in active listening: when we actively listen to stakeholders and then communicate our understanding of their needs, we can better address their issues and concerns. These are just a few of the ways the people of Sterling Staffing Solutions live the CARES model.

Servant Leadership

As mentioned, in the CARES model, the "S" stands for servant leadership. That's a role we take very seriously, but one that can take some explanation to be truly understood. We found that to be the case in a recent lunch-and-learn team-building session. We used an example of the human body—the head, neck, hands, arms, legs, and feet—and asked staff members which parts of the body represented the various roles in the organization. When it came to the roles of the company leadership, the inclination for everyone in the room was to point to the head, reflecting the belief that the executive team is the head of the body because those roles drive decision making and ensure that the company stays on track.

But the head does not represent the executives in an organization with servant leaders. The more appropriate body part is the feet, as servant leaders support the entire operation. They ensure that the organization stays well-grounded and stable and that staff has everything it needs to help move the organization forward. That's the basis of servant leadership. In the next section of the book, we will define this concept further.

A Leader's Mindset

Be the Last Person to Eat

When an individual enters service in the US military, usually they are at or near the lower end of the pecking order in terms of rank. Often they are an eighteen- or nineteen-year-old just out of high school, directionless and still lacking the maturity to make good decisions. Often they are barely able to be responsible for themselves, let alone anyone else.

The military understands this. It knows that its recruits are basically youngsters who need guidance to become mature men and women. They must be taught discipline, responsibility, and, for many, leadership skills. All that comes with time.

In the US Army, the branch of service that we served in, officers are the managers. The army states that officers "are tasked with making important decisions in stressful situations, and they are entrusted with the safety of the men and women under their command."[51] Many leaders of industry and of our nation once served as officers in the army.

There are four paths to becoming an officer in the US Army: (1) Army Reserve Officers' Training Corps (Army ROTC), (2) direct commission, (3) officer candidate school, and (4) the United States Military Academy (West Point).[52] The rank at which the graduate of these programs is commissioned into service is determined by the path and, in some programs, area of study and academic excellence.

Leadership training instills the understanding that leaders in the military serve soldiers. That means making sure that soldiers are trained in the skills they need to stay alive—at the end of the day, the role of the military leader is to save lives. The leader's role is to do everything possible to ensure that all the soldiers they lead make it safely home to their loved ones.

That kind of training changes a leader's point of view. When a leader looks at their role from the perspective that they must ensure that their soldiers—or in the civilian world, their staff—are trained to their very best in order to succeed, then ego is removed from the equation. That's why military leaders who are awarded for their actions often say, in essence, "I was just doing my job."

In the civilian world, the servant leader's role is no less critical: he or she must take care of the team to ensure their success and, in turn, the success of the organization.

The Role of the Servant Leader

As servant leaders, our approach is to ensure that everyone else is sufficiently prepared so that they can do their best every day. We don't focus on weaknesses. We focus on enhancing everyone's assets and helping them perform better in a role they already do well. We strategically put people in places where they are going to be successful, and then ensure that they have what they need to succeed.

In the military, officers eat last. Everyone else in the unit eats before the officers have their meal. The same concept applies to servant leaders in the corporate world. Staff must "eat first." When finances become a little slim, the staff must be paid before the leaders are paid. Staff must feel confident that the leaders are looking out for them and for the organization. They must believe their leaders are there to protect them and ensure that they have everything they need to help the organization succeed.

That "others eat first" concept is difficult to comprehend for some individuals placed in leadership positions. It was something that fighter pilots in World War II had trouble grasping until the Tuskegee Airmen were deployed. The Tuskegee Airmen was a fighter air unit given the mission to protect huge bomber aircraft during the war. Those bombers carried about a dozen airmen, and when they were sent into battle, fighter aircraft were sent to escort them and protect them from enemy fire. However, often those fighter pilots abandoned their escort mission for the sake of fame. Instead of staying with the bombers to fight off enemy aircraft, the escorts often peeled away from the bombers in pursuit of enemy aircraft. Their goal? A victory mark for their aircraft, which they earned with each plane they downed.

Once the enemy realized that the escort aircraft were leaving the bombers vulnerable, they would send out a few decoy fighters to engage the escort fighters in a sideline battle, and then send in aircraft to take out the bombers. By sheer numbers, the enemy was ahead: fighter planes carried far fewer solders than bombers, so while the American fighters were off pursuing one or two planes for the sake of glory, the bombers and their crews of a dozen or more men were being downed by enemy fighters.

That changed with the Tuskegee Airmen, who maintained the escort mission and earned numerous commendations for outstanding tactical air support.[53]

The Tuskegee Airmen demonstrated what it means to "eat last": by focusing on the bigger picture—the mission to save lives—they ensured that soldiers made it safely home.

In the same way, the servant leader must focus on the bigger picture—they must know and live the "why" to help the team believe and live the vision.

The servant leader must focus on the bigger picture—they must know and live the "why" to help the team believe and live the vision.

Traits of a Servant Leader

There are a number of traits that define a servant leader. These stem from the desire to build better people, a better product, a better company, and a better community.

Empathy for the Needs of the Workforce

As we've discussed, business leaders in today's world must be aware that employees often want to align with the values of their employer. Team members want to feel like they're a part of an organization and that it's one big family. Understanding this can help a company develop loyalty and grow a brand in a positive way.

A Sense of Stewardship

Today's employees are motivated to be in well-rounded positions with companies that not only provide growth opportunities for them as employees, but that also are investing in making a difference in the community. That investment has to make sense to them as well and must be consistent and constant.

A Team Player

Servant leaders are selfless, focusing on everyone else before focusing on themselves. They also work alongside their teams. When employees see a leader willing to be hands-on and go the distance to make goals happen, it's easier for them to believe the why and help the company move forward.

A True Doer, Not Just a Talker

Among millennials, there is also a level of accountability expected of leaders that is much different than in other generations. For these employees in particular, lip service won't do. They want to see that their leaders are consistently invested in what they say they're doing. Putting policies on paper isn't enough; those policies must be adhered to by every leader and every member of the team.

A Sense of Transparency

Being a servant leader takes more humility, because employees want transparency in their leadership. They want leaders who allow the entire team to feel empowered in the decision-making process to help the company grow.

That may even include knowing the financials. For instance, we currently have a goal of seventy thousand patient visits in one year, with the incentive of the team going on a cruise, so employees want to know how close we are to making that threshold. Similarly, one of our KPIs is to lower the average number of days it takes to collect payment—our days sales outstanding (DSO)—so they want to know how much money is being collected every week. Employees are taking an active role in the company's financials: they know our growth models and our financial goals for the year and they are incentivized to do so. That requires a level of transparency that may be uncomfortable for some leaders, but it's crucial for staff buy-in.

To engage employees, make them a part of the decision-making process. We do this by having open-discussion staff meetings. These meetings do not involve the CEO standing up at the head of the room telling the team, "This is how it's going to be." Instead, they involve issues being presented and the team actively weighing in on solutions, going through the pros and cons, and vetting the best possibilities. In the end, the leader in the room may narrow the solutions to those that are most viable, but the team usually selects the best option for the company.

There are some real pluses to this kind of group decision making. Allowing the team to be part of the process demonstrates the level of transparency they desire. It also builds the team, because everyone understands the goal and knows what they need to do to work toward it. And since it is a group decision, finger-pointing is lessened or eliminated altogether. If the decision results in a fail, then the group bears that burden together. If it becomes a win, then everyone participates in that success.

Fostering input from the team is simply using all of the tools that you have in your toolbox versus just trying to use the one hammer that you have in your hand. As leaders of our company, we often hash through an issue before presenting it to the group, and even come up with some potential solutions. But we still bounce the issue off the team because we want them to help vet it. We often throw out our own ideas and look for feedback, because everyone brings a different vantage point when it comes to decision making and problem solving. Our team members talk to our customers on a consistent basis, so they may have some insights that we don't have.

Fostering input from the team is simply using all of the tools that you have in your toolbox versus just trying to use the one hammer that you have in your hand.

Today's Workforce: It's Different

It's different dealing with millennials, because their motivation is atypical. For starters, they don't automatically have a sense of loyalty to a particular company. What drives them is work-life balance. Collectively, they actually have an entrepreneurial type of mindset. Going to work for a company and staying there for thirty years doesn't make a lot of sense to them. They want to work with a company that invests in their growth and success. If they don't feel like they're growing or improving their knowledge and skills, they don't feel they are giving their time to the right organization.

They are not interested in going to work every day at an eight-to-five job and being told what to do all day long. They need more. They want to know that their contributions are welcome and that their ideas are valued. Gaining their loyalty comes from making sure they understand that they are valued by the company and that they can be part of the company as it grows and expands into different ventures.

Millennials can make you feel like you're losing control of your own company. Entrepreneurs, especially, may find themselves disheartened. After all, many go into business to make their own decisions, define their own destiny, and not be limited by others in terms of what they're able to grow and become. They finally reach what they believe is a dream come true, and they don't want to answer to anyone. But what they find is almost the opposite—instead of having no one to answer to, they actually have to answer to everyone. Now they are responsible for keeping every stakeholder happy: employees, customers, creditors, vendors—everyone.

It takes an incredible amount of flexibility to answer to all the different stakeholders. In the end, however, final decisions—and the accountability for those—usually rest with the leader.

Leading Through Harvey

In the wake of Harvey, there were a number of people displaced due to water in their homes or in roadways, making them impassable. In spite of the damage and the hazards, patients still needed critical services. Although the rehabilitative services we provided clinicians were not matters of life or death, we still had to ensure that we provided care to those patients wherever they were located.

The trouble was finding those patients. We had no idea where they had relocated, and since they were more concerned about their flooded homes, they weren't worrying about missing a therapy appointment. In addition, many of our care providers, our clinicians, had also been displaced, and we didn't know where they were. When it came to locating them, we had to do more than seek them out and put them back to work. We also had to be cognizant of the emotions they were going through. Many of our clinicians were so overwhelmed by their personal situations and families' safety that it was very difficult for them to handle anything else. Managing both their personal situations and the situations of their patients required a special type of mental toughness.

What it boiled down to was connecting patients and providers to ensure that even amid a disaster like Harvey, people still received the care they needed.

Like many businesses, we could have just closed up shop for a few days and ridden out the chaos. But as servant leaders operating on the CARES model, discussed in the previous principle, we had to go outside the type of service normally provided.

Part of our efforts involved helping those members of our own staffing family get in contact with resources to put them back on their feet. We also started a fund for one clinician who had lost everything in the flood. In addition, the clinicians themselves went out of their way to help patients, taking funds from their own pockets to help those who needed assistance.

Harvey is perhaps an extreme example of what servant leaders do. But being part of the community, it is essential to take a role whether or not disaster has struck. Doing good in the community, we have found, truly does reward the business tenfold. That is something we discovered very early on when fulfilling our why.

When we opened Sterling Staffing Solutions, we made a concerted effort to be active in everything from supporting sports teams and school dances to membership in the local chamber of commerce. We wanted the community to know that we weren't here solely to do business—we wanted to take care of the community that was taking care of us.

Again, we consider the community one of our stakeholders, so our efforts must also work to blend the lines between public and private sectors to help strengthen the community. As a result, we have built a reputation as a company known for touching peoples' lives in everything we do.

But we can't do anything alone. That's the next step as a leader—learning to delegate tasks to others and also looking to mentors for guidance.

Teach and Be Taught

Michael Jordan was one of the best players ever in American professional basketball; he dominated the sport from the mid-1980s through the 1990s. As a member of the Chicago Bulls, he helped the team win six championship titles and was named most valuable player (MVP) five times during his career.

But even a superstar athlete like Jordan understood the value of a good coach and mentor. "My coach is everything," Jordan told filmmaker/writer Spike Lee in his book *Best Seat in the House*. Jordan was referring to his relationship with Phil Jackson, the renowned coach of the Bulls who led the team to those six championship titles. Jackson's contribution to the Bulls gave the team "the structure that elevated every player to his best possible self."[54]

Even Jordan, as great a player as he was, could not win a game all by himself; he needed a team, a fact that he notoriously struggled with at times. Fortunately, he was coachable, as he would later report: "My greatest skill was being teachable ... I was like a sponge. Even if I thought my coaches were wrong, I tried to listen and learn something."[55] That's the challenge for many entrepreneurs, business leaders, and people who want to excel. It can be tough to recognize when it's time to look to others for their expertise.

Everyone Needs Someone

Entrepreneurs are notorious for being very hands-on. In the start-up phase, the owner or entrepreneur may be hands-on with the day-to-day operations. From sweeping floors to answering the phone to making sales, they're doing it all. In an effort to stay profitable, they often want to hold onto to all the roles out of a belief that they are saving money.

But a business can only go so far if the primary leader is working in the business on all the day-to-day tasks, because any one person has only so much bandwidth. At some point, it's time to realize that by trying to do everything yourself, you're not saving money, you're actually losing money because you're doing tasks that are taking up valuable time—time that you could be devoting to more important pieces of the business.

There comes a point where the leader must work *on* the business, not *in* the business. They must become comfortable with the idea of delegating tasks to someone else. When you reach that point, your business will explode exponentially. When leaders spend their time guiding the business instead of sweeping the floors, they can be more visionary and analytical about the operation and its efficiencies.

---

*When leaders spend their time
guiding the business instead of sweeping
the floors, they can be more visionary
and analytical about the operation and
its efficiencies.*

It's easier to succeed with a team, and it's up to the leader to build that winning team. A few ways to begin deciding what roles to fill as you begin building that team include:

Make a List

As the leader, develop a list of your daily duties and then determine which of those are noncritical, non-CEO type tasks that can easily be delegated to someone else.

Place a Value on Your Time

As leader, place a dollar figure on your time—typically a CEO's wage should be around $150 to $250 per hour—and then determine whether the job being done is worth that hourly rate. Any task that is not worth that hourly rate and is not essential to your role as a leader should be delegated. Ultimately, the business owner should only be doing the essential tasks that will bring value to the business.

Be Honest With Yourself

Take the time to honestly reflect on your strengths and weaknesses. Then find individuals who are strong in the areas where you are weak.

Being comfortable with delegating to the right people means hiring people who are smarter than you. Don't be afraid to bring on talented professionals. If you are good at sales, but not so much at bookkeeping, then delegate the accounting portion of the business.

Look to Outsourcing

If there are some tasks that don't require forty hours plus benefits, outsource those to a company that can provide the few hours it takes to do the job. That way you're paying only for the specific services needed and not paying the salary, benefits, taxes, and liabilities that come with a full-time employee. For instance, hire a bookkeeper to take care of the company books and pay for that service on a monthly basis.

Once you decide what roles can be spun off, you can begin building and developing a team whose strengths balance out your own and that can help you build the business.

Transitioning to a Winning Team

Early on, the business may not be financially able to hire the highest quality staff. It won't have the budget to pay $100,000 a year for a top-notch manager who used to work for ExxonMobil. Start-ups don't often attract that kind of experience. That means being relegated to a certain level of personnel who may work really hard but may not have all the experience or exposure or even the intelligence that you really want long term.

After some time, the business reaches a transition point in its maturation where it goes through a phase of letting go of the initial personnel who were there from the very beginning and do not have the skill set to take the business to the next level.

That happens after the leader feels comfortable enough to delegate the skills and noncritical tasks to the right people. Once the roles are developed and the company grows, quality people can be brought in to fill those roles. Ensuring that you have the policies and processes in place can instill a bit of comfort during the transition, allowing newcomers to be more easily trained.

The goal is to move into a role that allows the business to continue running even when you're not around—the train won't leave the track if you're not behind the wheel 24/7. In spite of all the work it takes during start-up, few entrepreneurs go into business wanting to continually work twenty-hour days. A baker may start a pie shop because everyone loves his or her pies, and that love may be enough to support a bakery. But eventually the founder is going to tire of making 150 pies a day. That's when the recipes and techniques for baking those pies must be delegated to another, able baker, leaving the owner to pursue more outlets for their pies.

Delegating those technical pieces of the business to others can expand the bandwidth and even allow the company vision to outlive the founder. That's where we are with Sterling Staffing Solutions. Every therapist is equipped with our mission and vision, which broadens our bandwidth. Now instead of one therapist treating six or eight patients per day, nearly eight hundred therapists are making some five thousand patient visits per month. That has allowed us to aim for a goal of seventy thousand patient visits in one year.

Like the coaches of a basketball team, we are not out there running the plays. But we are on the sidelines orchestrating plays and making sure the team members are in the right positions and have the resources they need to score.

Building a balanced, sustainable team is a matter of identifying and developing good people. Every hire must be made with the expectation that the new employee will take some task off the leader's desk. Every role must also be a good cultural fit. Define your company's culture, and then look for those traits during hiring. The traits we look for include:

➡ **A strong work ethic**. We look for employees who worked through school, balanced multiple priorities, completed school in a shorter period of time, were active in extracurricular activities, and had a high grade point average. Honesty and integrity are also essential, although this may be difficult to determine at the time of the interview.

➡ **A positive attitude**. This is essential in health care—a positive attitude contributes to healing. But even in the office, a good attitude achieves far more than a gloomy one.

➡ **Able to handle pressure well**. Every business has adversity at some point, and the outcome often depends on how it is handled. The ability to handle pressure is crucial, especially in people who work directly with customers.

➡ **Dependability**. Clearly, the team needs to be able to rely on all of its members. When one doesn't carry their share of the load, it redistributes the workload onto others. You need team members you can rely on to do the task they are assigned.

➡ **Team oriented**. Every member of the team—even independent contractors—affects the other members, so you need someone who understands how their role fits into the bigger picture of the company.

➡ **Self-motivated**. Few managers have the time to hover over employees to ensure that they are doing their job. You need people who want to do the best job they can, not just because they're doing it for the company, but because it's in their DNA.

➡ **Flexibility**. In a small business environment, growth often occurs rapidly, and change is nearly constant. Your hires need to be open to change, to taking on multiple roles, and to adapting quickly.

The last thing you need or want is a team that must be micromanaged. Micromanaging ends up making the team less productive, because they're only going to do what you're asking or tasking them to do. Team members need to be given expectations and guidance, and then be allowed to excel. If you have the right people in the right positions, micromanagement won't be necessary, because they'll be self-motivated—they'll want to do a quality job because it's in them to do so.

Your team members need to feel they are trusted to do their job. Without that, they will never reach their full potential. Once you step back and let them do what they were hired to do, you will often find that they will give you more than you ever thought possible. As in any relationship, once there is trust, it blossoms.

The Value of Mentors

As a leader in business, you may feel you're at the top of the food chain. But there is always someone more successful who can provide you with guidance. We are big fans of having a business coach who can look at what we're doing in our business and give us guidance based on the industry standards and how business in general should be conducted.

Many very successful people tout the benefits of a good mentor or coach. Former tech executives Eric Schmidt (Google) and Steve Bennett (Intuit), renowned celebrity Oprah Winfrey, and former president Barack Obama have all spoken about the power of having a good coach to help advance their careers.[56] Virgin Atlantic, the British airline, would not have taken off without the mentoring of Sir Freddie Laker, according to the airline's owner, Richard Branson. [57] Thanks to mentoring and a $250,000 investment by Mike Markkula, Steve Jobs led Apple into the history books. Jobs then mentored Facebook founder Mark Zuckerberg, telling the youthful entrepreneur to reconnect with his mission and vision for the company. [58] And Microsoft founder Bill Gates credits Berkshire Hathaway chief Warren Buffett with helping him overcome adversity and think long-term. [59]

Having a mentor even at start-up can be very beneficial. A mentor is someone who has already been through what you're going through with your business, so they can help guide you through the process. They can help you grow professionally and personally and keep you from making some of the mistakes that every business owner makes.

Mentorship can actually occur in groups. There are numerous opportunities for business owners to meet on a regular basis to talk about issues that they have in business and brainstorm ideas for moving their business forward. One of those that we currently participate in is a strategic mastery group that meets monthly. It's essentially a book club for business owners and leaders. Each month, we read a book on leadership, self-empowerment, entrepreneurship, or other business aspects, and then we talk about how we can use what we read in a real-time, practical way.

Beyond the support and education we've gotten via group mentorship, we credit the actual start-up of the staffing company to Le Criss F. Smith, of ReThink Innovative Performance, a change management professional who helps businesses operate more effectively. Le Criss is a good friend of ours and knows both of us very well. As twins, we spent much of our lives doing things together, but when we began to define our own, independent pathways, Le Criss brought us together and pointed out how our strengths would complement each other perfectly in a business venture. He let us see that our skill sets were the perfect yin and yang.

Over time, we have also relied on other business coaches separately:

OUR PERSONAL MENTORS

Dr. Sterling L. Carter

I met Glenn Smith, founder of the Growth Coach and Glenn Smith Executive Coaching, through membership in the chamber of commerce, and he has been my business coach ever since. Glenn helped me understand how to value my time as CEO and, through his quarterly planner, I track my activities as a CEO. He helped me realize that some of my tasks needed to be delegated, and that really pushed me not to just work *in* the business, but to work *on* the business. His coaching and tools keep me accountable and have been invaluable in broadening my footprint and helping me take the business to the next level.

In truth, my brother Stephen is also a great business coach for me. He has an MBA and has owned and managed several businesses. So while I excel in knowledge about the health care industry, Stephen brings the business skill set to the table, which is not my strong suit. His advice became a turning point in my first business. As a marketing (and whiteboard) guru, Stephen helped me see that my advertising dollars were targeting the wrong demographic. Instead of marketing to consumers, who comprised around 40 percent of my business, I began spending my advertising dollars on meeting directly with doctors—the source of patient referrals. His advice helped me nearly double sales in one year.

I've always been an overachiever and workaholic. Left to my own devices, I'd probably work eighty to a hundred hours every week and do nothing else. But my wife, Crystal, has helped me understand that I must have some sort of work-life balance. She reminds me what's most important in life: It's not just about making as much money as possible. It's also about taking the time to enjoy life, spend time with the people I love, and just enjoy the fruits of all the hard work that I put in every day. She has also been an amazing sounding board, helping me find answers to questions and resolve concerns.

Crystal does all that for me in addition to her work in peri-operative medicine. Crystal uses her proven listening, communications, problem-solving, and strategic thinking skills at the world's number one cancer center to lead a team tasked with revamping and optimizing the hospital's operating room process, usage, and resources. With patient safety being the highest priority, she works with hospital executives to ensure that almost forty operating rooms, serving over thirty thousand patients, function at maximum efficiency. Additionally, she serves as a hospital subject matter expert and operations officer. In that role, she understands what it's like to work with surgeons and with patients dealing with cancer—two segments of the population that have elevated emotional needs and demands. Yet she juggles it all with admirable fortitude and grace.

Stephen Levi Carter, MBA

Jason B. Montanez, author of *Lead, Sell, Care as Easy as 123: It's Time to Get Back to Basics*, is a great business consultant who has mentored me and our team as a whole. He has helped us learn how to sell our vision and have others buy into it. His focus on team building, consistency, and demand for excellence has helped redefine our company culture. His enthusiasm and energy is infectious and has brought a welcome sense of urgency to our company's strategic mission.

Another mentor, Tyrone J. Dixon, founder of Mpulse Healthcare & Technology, has been through it all. He is a former manager and employer who has been instrumental in helping me avoid pitfalls. At one time, I went to him very gung ho about being an investor in a venture because I thought I could turn it around with my financial and marketing acumen.

Tyrone asked a lot of questions, trying to let me figure out for myself whether the venture was as great as I thought it was, and he very constructively tried to persuade me not to pursue the idea. Unfortunately I didn't take his advice, and I ended up wasting a lot of time and money. That taught me several valuable lessons: (1) find a mentor you can trust (someone who doesn't sugarcoat), (2) listen to them, and (3) always vet your ideas.

My wife, Daphane, has by far been my biggest mentor. She's a scholar, educator, and avid reader of books on leadership. As an executive of a major private charter school system, she is responsible for the academic success of more than thirty thousand youth throughout the state of Texas and influences the overall academic direction of the school system. But she also has an unparalleled influence on me.

While my brother Sterling credits me with having the business acumen that has helped the staffing agency succeed, my wife runs circles around me when it comes to leadership (she's the smart one in our family on that subject especially). She has a natural talent for hiring the right people, building and engaging teams, getting feedback from people to improve a task or skill, and knowing when and how to let someone go—all the knowledge that a great manager needs. And she shares that knowledge with me through very honest conversations that have helped me achieve real results.

We are also fortunate in that our wives have been mentors for us every day. They have been there for us from the beginning, providing support and guidance whenever needed.

Working with a Mentor or Coach

It may seem a bit daunting to find and then to work with a mentor, but as with every other aspect of your venture, do your homework and you will be rewarded.

If you already have a relationship with a successful business owner, you may find them to be a willing mentor. If they know you personally, they may be very interested in seeing you succeed. Having someone available to call up and ask questions can be a very valuable resource when opening the doors of a business.

If you don't have the luxury of a good relationship with a business mentor now, you can find business coaches online through resources such as LinkedIn. Often these thought leaders share their wisdom online, so you can gather a lot of good information free of charge before enlisting them for what is usually an hourly rate.

Here are some points to consider when seeking a mentor:

➡ **Decide what you need in a mentor.** Conduct some self-reflection to determine what you need to improve your business. Do you need to work on your leadership qualities or your leadership style? Do you need to know how to grow your business? Do you need help managing cash? Once you figure out what you need, locate a mentor who has built a company that excels in that trait.

➡ **Find a like-minded individual.** Look for a like-minded individual, someone who shares your philosophies or whose philosophies you are comfortable with.

➡ **Look for someone who doesn't sugarcoat.** Find a mentor who is authentic, transparent, and honest. You need someone who isn't afraid to tell you things you don't want to hear. You need someone who will be straight with you, even though those hard conversations are tough to hear but allow your company to grow and be better. Don't settle for someone who just wants to placate, who just wants to keep the relationship warm and fuzzy. That's not what you want or need from a mentor. You need someone who's going to challenge you throughout the relationship.

Mentors often give their time and energy free of charge, but they expect something in return—they expect you to value and take heed of their advice. Mentors like to be able to count others' successes among their own. It's their way of giving back for all the good that has come their way. Their attitude is similar to some personal trainers who work out with people at the gym: their biggest pet peeve is all the time and energy it takes to help a person change their fitness level and eating habits, only to have them six months later slide right back to where they began. It's the same with a mentor: they truly want you to succeed, and as the mentee, you have a responsibility to take heed of that advice.

As the mentee in a mentor-mentee relationship, refrain from doing all the talking. Instead, be prepared to listen actively. Come to the encounter prepared: Know exactly what you need help with, ask open-ended questions, and take notes. Listen for those nuggets of wisdom but be open to letting the mentor share them—that's where the real value is. Then be sure to implement the strategies and advice you are given.

As with delegating to others, when it comes to using a mentor, you need to be comfortable with the idea of letting go of that top-dog attitude a little. In order to help you with your business, a mentor will need to be in your space, to even be in your head at some point.

It can be difficult to expose your weaknesses, so you will need to decide how much confidential information you want to share.

Understanding how much you want to share will be especially true if you reach the place where you enlist the help of an advisory board. Members of these boards typically include top-notch individuals from different specialties, depending on your industry. That might include an attorney, an accountant, a social media guru, and others—such as a medical director in our case. During a meeting with the board, basically the company's "dirty laundry" is aired to generate feedback and insights that can keep the business on track. Such meetings can be pretty high pressure, but they are essential for holding the leaders accountable.

Your Turn to Mentor

Mentorship goes both ways. Once the business can be run without the leader hands-on 24/7, you can reach out and begin mentoring others to help them grow into leadership roles.

But also remember this: Mentorship happens all the time. It happens wherever you go in life. In a business start-up, it happens when employees see the great leaps of faith you take. It happens when family members see your commitment to succeeding. It happens when the community sees you giving back for all your good fortune. People often find those to be admirable traits, and they look up to you for having the courage those feats take. When you're selling the vision of the company, you're also selling yourself. When people see that kind of courage and conviction, when they see you doing something great, they want to join in that and make a difference for the long term.

We find that every relationship we have with our employees is a mentorship on some level. In daily conversations, in feedback on employee evaluations, in one-on-one meetings every other week where we sit down with the employees and let them to talk about issues they have, we provide feedback and mentor them to always improve. That open dialogue year-round is really a mentor-mentee relationship with employees that can help them—and the company—soar.

Where the Eagles Fly

I magine a group of workers trapped in a tunnel below Lake Erie after an explosion. That was the case on July 24, 1916, when water company workers hit a natural gas line during construction of a new freshwater line. As toxic gasses filled the tunnel, a local inventor was called to conduct the first real test of his award-winning product. Several years earlier, Garrett Morgan invented what is now referred to as a "gas mask," a device designed to help firefighters and others breathe in smoke- or noxious-fume-filled situations. Although his invention netted a gold prize at the International Exposition of Safety and Sanitation, it had yet to be tested in an extremely hazardous situation. When he heard of the explosion at Lake Erie, Morgan and his brother donned the masks and entered the tunnel, ultimately saving several of the trapped workers and turning the inventor and his mask into overnight successes. That call to use the mask in a dangerous, real-world situation proved its value and congealed its future as a lifesaving device. Morgan's invention would later be used by the US Army during World War I, where it would save thousands of American lives.[60]

It takes a considerable amount of dedication to succeed in any venture—just ask any inventor. Early on, being average may be enough to launch an idea, but it takes far more to keep that idea afloat. And it can take every ounce of effort you have to make that idea so distinctive, so successful that no others even come close. That's what most entrepreneurs are after—they want their idea to soar above all others.

If being phenomenal is your goal, then it's time to think bigger. It's time to get out of your own way and find ways to work smarter.

If being phenomenal is your goal, then it's time to think bigger. It's time to get out of your own way and find ways to work smarter.

Many people have great ideas, but they never take steps to make those ideas reality. Even if they start developing an idea, they don't seize the opportunity to take it to the next level, like Morgan did—he had so much faith in his product that he put his own life on the line. Too often, people fear that they lack the intelligence to launch an idea, much less see it become "an overnight success." But although intelligence is certainly celebrated today, it isn't the only factor in determining success. Success comes from not only outsmarting the competition, but also from simply outworking everyone else. In other words, work ethic trumps smarts.

Of course, it's easier to work hard if you love what you do. That goes back to finding and following your why, as we discussed in principle one, "Discover Your Niche." When you're working in your passion, you rise every day looking forward to going to work, and you excel because you are willing to go the distance. Being willing to work harder advances your knowledge and skills, because you are mastering your craft along the way. Often that means putting in more than a forty-hour workweek for more than a few years.

Once a venture is established, and another tier of managers is on board, it's time to look at how the working hours are spent. It's time to look at ways to be more efficient and productive. It's time to ramp up not only your own level of performance, but also to guide others, to really be the wings that lift the whole organization to its greatest heights.

Sustaining Success

As we related in the introduction, we came from a hardworking family. Our parents were born in Mississippi and grew up working on farms. That kind of upbringing required a strong work ethic, one that carried over to our generation and was honed by our military service.

In the military, you rise early and accomplish a lot in those hours before the rest of the world climbs out of bed. Remember the slogan, "In the army, we do more before nine o'clock in the morning than most people do all day"? That's us.

Army basic training started with wake up at four thirty every morning. If someone didn't wake up, the drill sergeant would turn over their mattress with them in it! Fifty soldiers in the platoon meant that sink, shower, and mirror time was a max of fifteen minutes. We had to be in formation for breakfast by five o'clock in the morning, and we were allowed fifteen minutes to eat. By five thirty, we were preparing for PT (physical training). PT lasted approximately an hour, and then we headed back to the barracks to clean up for class, which started at seven o'clock. All of the day's activities were that regimented, with breaks only for lunch and dinner. Around six o'clock in the evening, we headed back to the barracks to shine our boots, polish our metal, iron our uniform, and clean the barracks. Every so often, these activities would be interrupted by inspections.

An hour later at seven o'clock, the drill sergeant would drop in for about a half hour and give us specific instructions and feedback from the day. After he left, we had about an hour and a half to shower, change, write home, and socialize with barracks mates before lights-out at nine o'clock. At four thirty the next morning, we'd start it all over again.

Even though we are no longer in the service, we are still up very early, bouncing ideas off each other via email and text. It's not uncommon to put in several hours of work before we even arrive at the office. We spend those quiet, early morning hours planning the day, because by the time we arrive at the office there are typically many immediate demands on our attention. Those first steps in the door can inundate us and keep us working *in* the business, so we spend the very early hours working *on* the business.

That's what it takes to succeed. Establish your work habits and schedule, stick to them, and put in the time you need. Do all that and more, and you will reap the reward.

But as your company grows, your focus must shift from doing it all yourself to a more efficient and productive model. Simply working hard will no longer be enough to sustain the level of success you attained in the early years. Learning to maximize your output with the least amount of effort is essential as the company grows. You can always throw warm bodies at a problem to try to manage growth. But if a company of ten employees experiences 100 percent growth in revenue, is doubling the number of employees the best way to manage that growth? We've stopped at many points during the company's maturation to examine what we could do differently to avoid throwing more labor at a situation. Instead of just adding staff, we had to look at ways to reengineer existing processes and procedures to be smarter. We had to ask: How can we improve the process to make it more efficient, to make it easier for all parties involved? Because while leaders and owners may put in many extra hours to ensure the success of an organization, it is difficult to expect the same level of commitment from employees. We knew we had to find ways to engage and invest our people in the mission, vision, and purpose. And we did that, in part, by selling our vision (see principle five, "Sell Your Vision") and fostering the CARES model (principle six, "Lead with the CARES Model").

Work-Life Balance

At one point in our journey, we brought in a consultant to get feedback from the staffing agency team about how we were doing as leaders. The overall takeaway from the feedback was that we, the leaders, worked really hard and expected the same of team members. It was a message we received loud and clear.

SECOND OPINIONS—EVERYBODY NEEDS ONE

It's always a good idea to obtain a second opinion or input from an outside expert. It is not a sign of weakness for a leader to solicit the advice of an industry or subject matter expert. No one knows it all—so seek outside input as much as possible to help keep you on course and give you insight into your operations and your working manner. Second opinions are valuable assets in helping you avoid mistakes and pitfalls on the road to success.

As a leader, you may be driven by having more on the line. But employees often want—and deserve—more in the way of work-life balance. For them, considerations for their personal lives are part of the rewards these days of working with a company.

In fact, when moving into a role of overseeing a new tier of leaders, the owner or founder of a venture will still work hard *in* the business, but as discussed in principle eight, "Teach and Be Taught," the focus changes to one of working *on* the business.

Entrepreneurs in general tend to struggle with the idea that other people can be dedicated and have a good work ethic but also want to clock out at some point and go have a life. No one enjoys having a burned-out employee, and they should never be worked to that point. Obviously, the goal is to complete the job in a timely manner, but if it's a situation where a team has to work overtime every day or weekends on end to complete a task, then something needs to change. The situation needs to be viewed through a working-smarter lens to determine how to improve efficiencies.

Here are some ways to achieve maximum success with less effort:

Reorganize the Team

One solution is to reorganize team members. Align people into roles that better suit their strengths, then equip them with tools that offset their weak areas. That should allow them to focus on what they do well. Then implement measures to check the quality of their work to help them improve their weaknesses. Alternatively, there may be more value in determining a better role altogether—if someone is not technically savvy or detail oriented enough to fill a role, it may be less draining on resources to move them to another position.

Leverage Technology

Reengineering with technology is another way to work smarter. We've added in technology where possible so that instead of needing two people to do a job, we can now have one person with technological tools that allow them not only to perform the job with more work coming in, but to actually complete it more accurately and more easily.

Improve Processes

As a company matures, its processes tend to streamline, but sometimes that takes a concerted effort. Examine what processes look like today and how they could be improved. And be sure to update any documentation—revise any policies and procedures to reflect the new efficiencies.

Create a Comfortable Work Environment

Ideally, the workplace should be one that employees are excited to come to each day. We went through a phase where morale dipped. In exploring the situation, we found that a couple of very strong personalities on the team had created quite a bit of dissension. At one point, a couple of employees actually shared with us that they no longer enjoyed coming to work and only did so because they needed the money to take care of their families.

That's definitely not what we're looking for—it's counterproductive, as they were no longer engaged. When employees don't have their heart in the job, it can begin to affect customer service and other areas of the company.

In looking at ways to improve morale, we recognized that people wanted to also celebrate their personal lives, not just their professional wins. They enjoy celebrating major life experiences such as getting married, having children, buying homes, and more. They also very much appreciate when those milestones are recognized by their employer. When someone has a child, a small gift goes a long way. When someone buys a new home, a housewarming gift is a small gesture that means a lot.

Occasionally, employees also need time off to mark events in their lives. Paid time off is rarely denied, and employees are encouraged to take the vacation that is allotted to them for the year and not bank a lot of hours. That's the point of time off, to keep them from overworking.

Invest in Employee Growth

Investing in opportunities for continuous education and growth can help the company be stronger and smarter. We invest in a program that provides training through annual memberships that give employees unlimited access to skills advancement and self-improvement courses. We also identify areas where we want them to grow and have them take a course once a quarter. We want to ensure that we're giving the team the training they need to continue to perform at their best.

Employees who don't have an ownership stake in the company will have motivations different than yours for their dedication to your company's and their own success. That's why it's crucial to understand what drives people to be passionate and loyal for as long as they are with a company. That goes back to servant leadership—understanding your employees and what motivates them and recognizing that they have different motivators. If you can connect with them and speak to them in their language, they will put in the value that is needed.

Try to discover their "why"—why they are connected to the organization, what they want in life—and then give them encouragement. It's easy to become disconnected because you are so hooked on your day-to-day tasks and routine that you forget to have one-on-one meetings or to simply check in and see how they are doing. But a simple "Hey, how was your weekend?" or "How's your family doing?" often speaks to their why.

That's important even if an employee is ultimately only short-term. Let's face it, for many employees your venture may not be the final stopping point in their career, and that's okay. For instance, if they want to become business owners themselves, they may benefit from a mentor. For us, since part of our why is to mentor others, supporting their why ultimately helps us achieve ours.

Elevate with Quality

When everyone works harder together, it can elevate the company to that next level. Like two wings of an eagle, there are two components involved in keeping an organization on track: quality and ethics. Let's look at the first "wing"—quality.

Quality begins with hiring the right staff. Period.

As discussed in principle eight, "Teach and Be Taught," employees hired when starting a company tend to be those at the lower end of the salary spectrum. But to sustain quality for the long-term, the amount of money saved by hiring mediocre employees for low wages versus top-notch employees for more competitive wages can be significant. The right employee can literally produce at least two to three times more high-quality work than a poor-performing employee. That's known as performance differential, or the performance difference between hiring an average employee and a superstar employee.

> ## Quality begins with hiring the right staff. Period.

Companies like Google, Microsoft, GE, Apple, and Yahoo have all found a minimum of double-digit performance differentials between superstars and average employees. In fact, at Google, the average employee generates over $1 million in revenue each year. Yes, you read that correctly: one employee equals $1 million annually for Google. What's more, Google's top software developers, or "purple squirrels," literally bring in $300 million annually for the company. Google has found that a top performer produces three hundred times more revenue than an average employee. So, although an average software developer would typically be compensated around $145,000 in Silicon Valley including salary, stock, and bonuses, a Google top software developer could make as much as $850,000 per year in salary, cash, and bonuses. That's an ROI of more than 35,000 percent for a top performer versus 690 percent for an average performer.[61]

Google top performer: $300 million / $850,000 = 35,294 percent

Google average performer: $1 million / $145,000 = 690 percent

The long-term gain in hiring a Google top performer *far* outweighs the short-term benefit of a lesser cash outlay for hiring an average employee. It's an easy decision.

In industries like health care, the impact of quality can be much more critical, since not being exceptional could literally decide the life or death of a patient. You can't put a dollar value on the life of a human being. In fact, a study by researchers at Johns Hopkins estimated that medical errors are one of the leading causes of death in the United States, ranking third behind heart disease and cancer, and are among the top two causes of death according to the Centers for Disease Control and Prevention.[62]

What is unique about health care compared to other industries is that the oversight is not necessarily at the point of contact. Typically, care is provided in a one-on-one situation between a clinician and the patient. The oversight regarding quality care by the clinician is accounted for in the documentation. As a measure of quality then, the documentation is very carefully scrutinized to ensure the documents can tell the story and that the desired output has been achieved. Without a supervisor being there to actually witness what happened, the documentation needs to paint the picture of the visit.

Like many industries, then, quality must look at both the people side and the administrative side, and we make a conscious effort to excel on both sides of that equation. We want customers to know that they can rely on us for quality care of their patients and quality documentation that ensures that care was delivered and that they can bill appropriately and avoid audits or other issues from their oversight committees.

Stay Aloft through Ethics

What truly ensures the success of an organization and hammers home its reputation are the ethics that drive people. However, quality assurance measures are also crucial in any business to ensure the highest ethical behavior.

In health care, clinicians take an oath to do the right thing by their patients. In this industry, especially with those professionals who provide hands-on care, a certain number of continuing education units (CEs) on ethical behavior are required each year. Obviously only the clinician, the patient, and the good Lord above know what really takes place during a home health visit. There's a lot riding on the clinician to truly make a difference.

In addition to an ingrained belief in high ethical standards, part of what keeps clinicians honest is that complaints about flaws or deficiencies in care that are reported to the appropriate regulatory body are taken very seriously, and each one is fully investigated. As part of the hiring process, clinicians undergo criminal and clinical background checks to see whether there have been any reports from a care standpoint. Any dings in a clinician's record are discussed in depth with the clinician to determine whether or not to move forward with the hiring. That is part of the screening process, which also includes in-depth discussion of the company's expectations, setting the tone for a quality therapist who provides ethical care. We vet, screen, and interview new clinicians. Then, during orientation, we talk about the importance of quality documentation and let the clinician know that their notes will undergo a quality assurance check.

We also make random calls to patients to check on the care being provided, and we're constantly in contact with our customers, the home health agencies, to see how our contract therapists are doing. We also receive feedback from patients. Through these measures, we can stay on top of contract care providers. When we do have a contractor who is not working or behaving to our standards of quality and ethics, we can remedy the situation very quickly.

Of course, we also use technology for quality assurance. As discussed in principle four, "Rome Wasn't Built in a Day," our electronic medical records system has electronic patient signature functionality. The system uses global positioning to capture the physical location where the signature was taken. When the patient signs the signature sheet on the clinician's tablet or smartphone, the time, date, and location are recorded. That is then compared to the address of the patient, so a clinician cannot forge a signature from another location. The system also helps clinicians with the administrative portion of their role, as it requires them to obtain that signature on site rather than completing the patient paperwork later.

Admittedly, ethics can be a challenge in any industry when people are intent on helping others. It can be difficult to say no when a patient or customer has a request outside the scope of providing service or that may border in some way on a company's standard of ethics.

But in health care, strong ethics are so ingrained that it becomes easier to say no. That became very apparent when we started this business. From the health care perspective, the ethics were clear-cut, but at times, the business perspective—the profit-driven side— opened the door to ethical discussions. In the end, ethics won.

Medicare fraud is prevalent in the health care industry, even though such fraud is a federal offense with some very big repercussions. That makes for heavy concerns about making sure everything is done the right way—no shortcuts, nothing substandard. Even an investigation can seriously mar a reputation in this business. That's why we walk a straight line when it comes to ethics—we won't give in to illegal or fraudulent requests and often walk away from questionable business. We don't want to work with companies that are willing to do something unethical or fraudulent. Not only is it wrong, but that kind of behavior can leave an ethical company high and dry when the unethical company goes out of business owing it money. We've become savvy enough to look at clients' operational tactics, and if we see they're doing business in a questionable manner, we take the nearest exit—we don't want to become caught up in their bad decisions.

In a situation like ours, an unethical decision by a contractor that we staff can ultimately hurt the contractor, our company, and our client. If the need for investigation arises, in most situations the patient looks to the home health agency for a resolution. Medicare would also investigate the agency as the licensing entity. In fact, investigators of Medicare fraud cases often start at the top and go through all the contractors, subcontractors, and employees—every person affiliated with the person or organization suspected of committing the fraud. No business, no unethical employee, is worth being caught up in that spider web.

Ethics also involves doing what is appropriate with regard to customer service. In health care, that means following protocol, which is one reason we vet contractors so heavily. It can be frightening and even dangerous for a patient to have a provider come into their home who does not ultimately have their best interests at heart. If, for instance, a therapist has a patient bear weight on a leg too soon after a total hip replacement, against protocol, everyone involved in providing care can potentially be held liable for any damage that arises.

In the end, having high ethics will weed out the bad clients, employees, and practices in a business. It will help a company be more respected and help it succeed.

Sterling Staffing Solutions is well respected because clients, employees,

> **Steps to Ensure an Ethical Company, Processes, and Employees:**
>
> 1. Effectively screen for the right employees, people who are driven by high ethics.
>
> 2. Establish quality assurance measures and processes to keep employees and companies accountable.
>
> 3. Immediately take steps to weed out any companies or employees that exhibit poor ethical behavior.

contractors, and vendors can rely on it to do the right thing. It is a company owned and managed by a health professional who has an insight into what's best for the patients. That has been one of the keys to success, especially in health care, which is a small world. Everybody knows everybody, and reputation is everything.

Everybody knows everybody, and reputation is everything.

We hold our employees very accountable for any missteps or mistakes. If there is a mistake or a misstep, we stop, sit down, and talk about how it happened, the lessons learned, and how to avoid it in the future. This is not done in a way to beat up employees, but to help them recognize that we should be smart enough to catch these kinds of mistakes. It's imperative that we catch errors before our clients do; it would be unprofessional to do otherwise. But if there is an issue, we are not afraid to reach out to a client or to admit that we've made a mistake. We recognize that the misstep is ours as a team; resolving the issue means revisiting our processes and standard operating procedures to determine whether it was training or a process that was at issue and not just human error. What could we have done better, what steps in the process could we have changed to catch the issue sooner or avoid it altogether?

That's our situation in this highly regulated industry. But many organizations are driven to practice high ethics in business. Some of those that have repeatedly been recognized for their ethical standards include:

➡ **Volvo Cars.** Twice named one of the world's most ethical companies, Volvo Cars has established internal and external programs and training to mitigate unethical or illegal practices throughout the company and in its interactions with business partners.[63]

→ **Dell Inc.** Named one of the world's most ethical companies for the fifth consecutive year in 2018, Dell has a council composed of executive leaders and department heads that oversees risk and compliance and guides strategic decision making.[64]

→ **Microsoft.** For the eighth straight year in 2018, the company that the world relies on to keep data secure made the list of the world's most ethical companies. The company sees trust as key to its ethical practices, and it guides its employees by reminding them of three steps to follow when faced with a complex situation: (1) pause and listen to your gut, (2) think about whether the approach is consistent with the company's culture and values, and (3) ask for help from a manager.[65]

→ **Grupo Bimbo.** The Mexico-based baking and snack product maker and distributor was named most ethical for its integrity and belief that high ethics builds trust, which it views as its most important asset.[66]

A stellar reputation can be crucial for digging out when something negative occurs. It can also be a source of pride for employees or people representing the organization, making it easier to champion the company. When a company produces quality and is known for its ethical standards, it's easier for people to be brand ambassadors, because they believe in the product and the service.

POTENTIAL
PITFALLS

Stay Hungry

Borders was a brick-and-mortar bookseller that at one time had nearly eight hundred stores and over eleven thousand employees. Along with the still-viable Barnes & Noble, Borders essentially invented the megastore book business. The company built a reputation for having thousands of books of every variety in a single store. But the company made a critical mistake—it misjudged the impact of digitization.

In the mid-1990s, Borders invested heavily in CD and DVD sales just as the music industry was going digital. At the same time, their main competitor, Barnes & Noble, was pulling back on in-store stock, beefing up its online sales, and developing its own reader for e-books, which were fast entering the market. Instead of going head-to-head with Barnes & Noble in the digital book space, Borders decided to outsource its online book sales to Amazon—which basically equated to handing over the keys to the kingdom.

In 2011, Borders closed its remaining four hundred stores while Amazon quickly grew beyond just the sale of digital books to the sale of *everything* online. And of course, the rest is history. Amazon is now the largest internet retailer in the world, boasting nearly $178 billion in revenue in 2017.

All Grown Up? Think Again

Once a business reaches a level of success, it's easy to be tempted to relax a little. But that can complicate the challenges of doing business. Whatever the venture, staying ahead is a matter of staying in tune and not riding on past successes. Even though we are a mature company with many successes to our name, we know that in this ever-evolving industry, every day is a new day with new challenges that must be met head-on.

The greater the success of your company, the more people will begin to notice and study your success. Your competitors know that it is easier to start a company by simply improving upon an already successful idea. So, you must be always prepared for the lion lying in wait. Your competition is waiting for an opportunity to pounce and take over your position. Innovation most happens when a new company imitates its competition and simply improves the service offering. So, if you are not improving daily, you are being left behind by your competition. Corporate executives and business schools tend to focus solely on innovation.[67] But when starting a company, your competitors are most likely tweaking your existing idea as it is both easier and more profitable than creating something from scratch.

Take UPS versus FedEx. UPS is a one hundred-year-old parcel express delivery company where, up until recently, the majority of their package deliveries were made via ground delivery. FedEx, opened in the early '70s, is an express delivery behemoth that took the UPS model and just tweaked it. FedEx express delivery is primarily by air. FedEx saw an improvement was needed in getting supplies such as medicine and computer parts delivered expeditiously. In 2017, FedEx grossed $60.3 billion in revenues versus UPS's gross revenue of $65.84 billion. FedEx is very close to passing UPS in a relatively short period of time. Even mature companies cannot afford to sit back and rely solely on reputation. Even the best brands must stay hungry if they are to compete against a constant flow of up-and-comers.[68]

How to Stay Ahead

There are five areas that tend to be overlooked as an organization matures. Without constant attention to these, challenges can arise and complicate an organization's ability to stay ahead.

Lack of Structure

The structure of a company often changes as it matures, and measures must be taken to ensure that it continues to operate effectively as it evolves. In the early days of a start-up, one or two people typically multitask all that needs to be done. There are no silos, because when there is only one person, that person owns all the information in the company, and when there are two people, little forward momentum occurs unless there is communication. When we started, we had a handful of team members who did a multitude of different tasks, but the quality of the care provided was not what we needed it to be.

We started isolating activities to allow members of the team to very clearly focus on specific areas. What we quickly discovered was an increase in quality in those areas as team members started to focus on a specific task.

As a company grows, it begins to be structured into departments. Those departments focus on quality within their area of responsibility, but without communication across the organization, quality as a whole can suffer.

The challenge comes in the handoff between departments. Often, when the structure of a company begins to departmentalize, "not-my-job" scenarios tend to pop up. That's how errors happen—when employees are unclear about their role in a process, components of an activity can fall through the cracks. By identifying those tasks and activities that move from one area of the company to another, you can put quality procedures in place to ensure a smooth handoff. That can also help maintain a team mentality and avoid having large numbers of independent contributors who do not understand their piece of the whole or the value that their role or department brings to the table.

Lack of Proper Marketing

When a company has matured, it's easy to overlook the value of marketing. That can be a mistake that leaves the door wide open for competitors. Take high-end automakers, for instance. Outside of product placement in movies, Jaguar advertisements are rarely targeted at the masses. But brands like Audi, BMW, and Mercedes are far more commonplace these days. What changed? These brands have altered their models and marketing to target world changes—ranging from environmental awareness to a shrinking market of middle class buyers.[69] And they have done so without compromising their brands or sacrificing their profit margins.

If you're not marketing, you're allowing a potential competitor to come in and take over market share. Once you establish a brand, you must keep it in the game, and that means being dedicated to ongoing marketing efforts.

> *If you're not marketing, you're allowing a potential competitor to come in and take over market share.*

Staying ahead of the competition also means continually redesigning products, product delivery systems, or services.

Companies that don't see value in marketing often look at that part of the budget as the first to go when considering expenses. That can happen when a company is doing well and decides to look for ways to improve efficiencies; it can also occur when a company reaches what is perceived as a level of comfort. But in business, assuming all is well at any time can be dangerous. Just because a few great clients are sending a significant amount of business your way doesn't mean something won't change tomorrow.

Marketing on a consistent basis can produce a pipeline of clients, potentially diversifying a portfolio to help it weather any storms.

Again, remember from principle four, "Rome Wasn't Built in a Day" that marketing is both internal and external—every employee should act as an ambassador to help market the company every day, whether to each other, to existing or potential clients, or to the public as a whole.

Lack of Delegation

As a mature company, there is undoubtedly at least one tier of management for the leaders to delegate to. As the company matures even more, it is up to those individuals to begin delegating tasks. That's when those stars mentioned in principle four, "Rome Wasn't Built in a Day" come into play.

In peeling back the layers on huge, successful organizations, one common denominator is the percentage of star employees. Stars are those few employees who produce the majority of work in a company, sort of the 80/20 rule—stars are the 20 percent of employees who produce 80 percent of the work required to move the company to the next level. Look to stars when delegating tasks. Identify those very smart, very savvy employees who can handle additional tasks. Give them what you can to keep them engaged, without overloading them. Then let them spread their wings. If you've hired people smarter than you, then delegating challenging tasks that keep them engaged should be easy enough to do.

Lack of Relevancy

Start-ups tend to fail within three to five years, so being past the five-year point might indicate the company is in a good place. But it's still important to stay focused and nimble—those are key in changing with the times and staying relevant. Never give up on being the very best at what you do. Growth and improvement do not always mean the company grows in size; the company may simply become better at what it does until it is the very best. That means improving the quality of products, services, efficiencies, and any other element of operations.

Never give up on being the very best at what you do.

We have used technology to improve and expand operations. By broadening our bandwidth, we were able to add three more cities to our operations without a physical office in those locations. And since we did not hire many additional staff members, our expenses leveled out while profits continued to rise. That's one way to improve operations and grow market share—by improving efficiencies without a lot of additional expense.

As we write this book, one company that has had more than its share of challenges is Snapchat. Once the darling of the online app world, the company saw its stock plummet by $1.3 billion following a single post by celebrity Kylie Jenner stating she no longer opened the app.[70] The drop in stock followed the launch of a redesign that more than 1.2 million of Snapchat's 24 million users signed a petition urging the company to rethink.[71] A month later, its stock dropped another $800 million after the company was criticized by the pop star Rihanna.[72] And all of this is in the face of stiff competition from the fast-growing Instagram app.[73] Whether Snapchat will survive is yet to be seen, but one thing is certain: the company is struggling to stay relevant in an online world of fickle consumers where one disgruntled customer can, with just a few clicks, turn into millions of lost customers.

If you are in a situation where you have clients with that much control over your value, you're going to have to work really hard to keep them happy or you need to diversify what you're doing. In principle five, "Sell Your Vision," we discussed ways to combat negative online feedback. In a case as drastic as Snapchat's, even an apology didn't work with Rihanna, but that doesn't mean a goodwill gesture isn't worth the effort. In the face of such negative publicity, consider reaching out to the individual to talk with them about how their feedback is being used to change the way the business operates.

We've actually done just that. We took the feedback we received, made some changes, and then went back to our clients and told them what we now do differently.

Beware of the comfort zone. Although a business might reach a point of stability, it's dangerous to become too comfortable. You must stay focused and continue to put the work in. If you keep your eye on the road and push every day, your business will continue to move and grow. But if you try to put the business on cruise control, it can take a lot longer to get back on track after you miss a few exits.

If you're not out for more business or you're in a place where the company is a size deemed manageable for the time being, you can still enhance internal operations to strengthen the company in preparation for things to come.

Stagnancy

Stagnancy occurs when a company fails to stay on top of trends or pay attention to their industry and marketplace. Go back to the business plan, look at long-range goals, consider expanding, work on soaring with eagles (see principle nine, "Where the Eagles Fly"), and think about diversifying.

Here are some other ways to stay ahead of the competition:

- **Subscribe to trade journals and industry magazines**. If you are not already reading all you can about your industry, consider starting a few subscriptions to help put yourself in the loop about changes and trends.

- **Stay on top of your newsgroups and news feeds**. Find relevant news feeds and make it a habit to read them each day. Save those articles that warrant a closer read or may serve as a resource later on.

- **Join organizations**. Whether it's the local chamber, area industry association, or other group, joining an organization or two can present networking opportunities to help you remain relevant and stay in touch with goings-on in your area and your industry. Our membership in our local chamber helped us connect with attorneys, accountants, business coaches, and other resources.

- **Attend conferences**. From national events to local gatherings, conferences in your industry or complementing industries can help you stay informed while expanding your network of colleagues.

- **Share your talent**. If you are not already involved in a leadership role in the industry or in the community, look at ways you and your team can be involved. Find organizations looking for leaders as board directors. Here again, these provide networking opportunities while allowing you to share your talent in a leadership role.

Again, the impact of the millennial generation is a craving for constant improvement, constant ways to strengthen their skill set. Creating programs and processes that focus on continuous improvement benefit the company by having better employees, products, and services, but is also crucial for retention. One way we are continually strengthening our culture is by having a consultant meet with our team once a month to improve teamwork. We are big proponents of investing and improving the skills of our employees and of our company, because we know that ultimately that's going to lead to our continued success. It will help keep us ahead of the competition.

The key is to avoid being too comfortable, because at some point a competition or a disaster may present itself. Will you be ready?

Prepare for Storms

The story of the days leading up to Hurricane Harvey is one that we've seen in Houston nearly every hurricane season. A storm begins building in the Atlantic and its path is tracked every day, every hour. Until it leaves the Atlantic, however, the people of Houston more or less go about their day. Once it enters the Gulf, some people may prep for the storm by picking up supplies, filling up their car with gas, and prepping for the temporary, short-term impact that a low-level threat of a storm may actually produce. Over the years, people have become desensitized to weather-related threats, because amid a whole lot of media frenzy, the anticipated weather events often end up being little more than rain showers and maybe surf warnings at worst. In short, native Houstonians have an attitude of "been there, done that"—it's not really that big of a deal.

Aerial photograph of the destruction caused by Hurricane Harvey.
Source: South Carolina National Guard

Hurricane Harvey, of course, devastated Houston. It was literally not just a once-in-a-lifetime natural disaster—it was a once-in-a-thousand-years flood. Harvey was one of the most expensive natural disasters in US history: $125 billion of damage.[74] It left nearly the entire city underwater, and most residents and businesses were not prepared. More than one million vehicles were totaled, 203,000 homes were damaged, and 80 percent of all Houston businesses were affected.[75]

Sterling Staffing Solutions was one of those companies. We found ourselves struggling to figure out a way to counteract or mitigate the potential risk on a number of different fronts. We had displaced employees, clinicians, and patients. Critical care needed to be provided to a number of patients, but we didn't know where those patients were, because their homes were flooded out. Even those employees and clinicians who weren't displaced were immobilized because of impassable streets.

For the first time, we were challenged to figure out ways to keep the company operating. We had never even considered a backup plan should a disaster with the impact of Harvey occur. As the storm continued to dump on Houston, we had to consider how to reorganize: Could our team work from home? Should we find a secondary location to operate from? In addition to the logistical impact, we were dealing with the emotional impact of dealing with people who weren't mentally prepared to move forward because they were dealing with so much at one time.

Similar scenarios often happen in business. Companies tend to reach a place where they appear to run on autopilot. An organization may even reach the top of the heap in its industry and feel impervious to any threat from the competition. It may have survived while other start-ups came and went by having policies and procedures in place, leaving it to believe that no new threats will arise. It may have a team that operates as a well-oiled machine which makes it seem that if an issue were to arise it would be handled without worry.

Offense—the Best Defense

The best defense is offense—although a defensive plan can help the company recover when disaster occurs, an offensive plan can help avoid disaster in the first place.

Taking an offensive stance to combat problems can mean many things. For us, it meant diversifying our service offerings. As we shared in previous principles, we started by offering staffing only for physical therapy clinicians. We then recognized other niche markets that could benefit from staffing in the home health environment. We began staffing for occupational and speech therapy, and then for social work, nursing, medical doctors, and home care aides.

We started looking at staffing hourly employees, temporary-to-permanent, and even permanent positions. We recognized that this business is primarily driven by Medicare, and we realized the financial risk of having a business built on the reimbursements of a federal government–funded program. So, we transitioned into providing therapy and nursing to hospitals and school districts. By looking at hospitals and schools, two market segments that were less heavily regulated as home health, we were able to expand our bandwidth.

After having success in those areas, we decided to look even further beyond our base market. In Houston, one of the major industries besides health care is oil and gas. Since the other half of our expertise is in that field, it was a fairly smooth transition to move into that area.

Then with the success of the nursing placement education as well as oil and gas industries, we discovered staffing needs among professional, technical, administrative, and light industrial employees, so we added those positions to our portfolio. We then expanded our coverage from only Houston to all major cities in Texas and Oklahoma.

The bottom line is that with a diversified service offering in various geographic regions, we have reduced our risk of being negatively impacted by any disaster, natural or man-made. By taking careful steps and recognizing an opportunity for growth when it arises, any venture can measurably diversify and reduce disaster-related risks.

Preparing for the Storm

Preparing for the storm is about thinking short- and long-term about all the negative things that could potentially occur, meanwhile developing a backup plan for what can be put in place now to cushion a negative impact or avoid it altogether. Use the six o's technique, as mentioned in principle four, "Rome Wasn't Built in a Day" to help determine potential risks for a company:

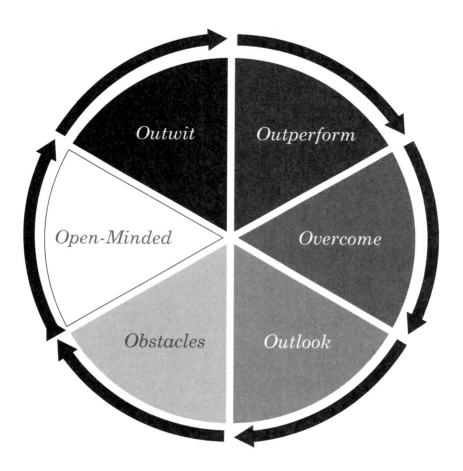

Again, bring together the entire team and look at the six o's from internal and external perspectives. Remember that no idea is a bad idea when brainstorming the six o's, and look for five main points for each "o." Finally, create actionable steps for every component in each category and use them as part of goal setting.

Disaster Comes in Many Forms

Make no mistake, it doesn't need to rain a deluge for days on end to be classified as a disaster that can harm an organization. The following are some pitfalls to prepare for before they occur.

Cash flow is always a potential issue in business, and not just for paying out settlements. The downfall of many businesses is that the company grows so fast that it runs out of business—it hasn't maintained its expenses, and it equates a high amount of revenue to profit. But that's not always the case. When growth occurs, typically expenses grow. That can lead to overspending—including spending yourself out of business.

That can also happen when trying to manage fluctuating business cycles. Professional lives are the same as personal: the business needs three- to six-months' worth of savings in case revenue temporarily subsides. That savings can help cover expenses until business picks up again.

It can be daunting in the beginning to accumulate three to six months of cash, so start with a goal of setting aside one months' worth. Then build that to two months, then three months, with the ultimate goal of six months of savings.

A rainy day fund may be a business savings account, a line of credit from a bank, an SBA loan, or, ideally, cash or some form of low-risk, liquid asset such as an interest-bearing savings account, a certificate of deposit (CD), or a municipal bond. No one wants to have cash laying around, so ideally find a highly accessible investment vehicle that offers some type of return.

Keep in mind the growth of the company when putting aside savings: while three to six months of savings may have covered expenses last year, this year it may not be enough.

Staffing Ebb and Flow

As we shared in principle four, "Rome Wasn't Built in a Day," we know firsthand the challenges of having the capacity to handle growth and the demands of new business. It's challenging to balance the number of employees with the amount of work coming in. Without enough employees, you can't deliver products and services as promised, yet if you overstaff, you face laying off people when business takes a dip. In our case, it was an influx of referrals that left us unable to deliver.

Again, it's critical to plan ahead. If the goal is to double sales, then even if technology drives that growth, it will likely take some additional staff to support it. And it's better to be proactive than reactive when it comes to staffing—it's tough to meet the demands of a multimillion-dollar contract with a staff accustomed to the workload that a half-million dollars in annual revenue brings. In the end, quality may suffer, and that can negatively impact reputation and even future business.

A great way to fill employee needs is with utilizing a temporary staffing agency. Typically, a staffing agency can place a skilled candidate in your business in a very short period of time. The benefit is that you can use this contractor for as long as needed and terminate the contract if your current demands decrease. The staffing agency will typically handle all benefits and tax burden for the contractor which decreases your overall financial burden. In addition, if the candidate is someone that you want to keep on a permanent basis, you will typically have the ability to convert the position from temporary to permanent. In contrast, if the contractor is not a good fit, you are easily able to send the contractor back to the agency and request a new one.

We have also used student interns and volunteers to assist when times are busy. This is a great way to have extra help at low cost to no cost. In addition, if the intern or volunteer turns out to be a great potential hire, you can easily convert them to an employee and you are already familiar with their work ethics and how they work in your company culture.

One other tactic is to hold onto résumés of good potential employees that you have interviewed in the past. You will want to keep a file that you can quickly turn to and make calls to these individuals when you have a critical need.

The Sudden Departure of a Critical Employee

Although it seemed that even a powerhouse like Apple might not survive following the demise of its visionary leader, Steve Jobs, the company has managed to continue on. At the time of Jobs's demise only weeks after stepping down in 2011, Apple was worth around $350 billion.[76] In 2018, it is valued at nearly a trillion dollars.[77]

As mentioned in principle five, "Sell Your Vision," losing a key employee can be a setback—and when it's a leader as influential as Jobs, "setback" may be an understatement. In addition to the time and expense of bringing in a replacement, providing them training, and having them become familiar and comfortable in their role, there are concerns about the exiting employee. While Tim Cook had previously filled in for Jobs, his ability to take over the leadership role full time was a topic of great speculation. Although the company's stock dipped 2.25 percent in the wake of Jobs's departure, it recovered in the face of record holiday sales that year.[78]

Most organizations won't face such a dramatic exit as the loss of a deathly ill CEO. But just how do you handle the sudden departure of an employee in a key role? The answer: processes, processes, processes. Even the roles and responsibilities of the top positions must be part of an organization's documentation. It is absolutely detrimental to operate otherwise; to do so could leave the company in a bind if a key employee exits and no one has a clue what they did on a day-to-day basis. The roles and responsibilities of every member of the team must be documented.

Damage control is also essential when a key employee leaves. All passwords must be changed. All mail and email must be rerouted. All business property such as keys, key cards, computers, and other items must be retrieved. One way to ensure that everything is returned is to hold onto any personal property left behind by the individual and make the last paycheck available for pick-up upon return of the company's proprietary property.

Another consideration: unemployment taxes. When an employee is let go, they can request unemployment reimbursement. That increases the unemployment tax rate on a business, which can be significant and even affect the bottom line.

To protect against aftereffects from a firing, keep a paper trail on every problem employee. Verbal conversations with employees about their behavior do not hold weight with the unemployment office. Problems must be documented and filed in the employee's personnel file—that documentation includes emails. These measures can help support your case should the employee file for unemployment, or worse, attempt to sue for unfair treatment. The subject of human resources is vast, but the Society for Human Resource Management is an outstanding resource, with a wealth of public information on the subject at www.shrm.org.

Planning for the sudden departure of a critical employee—or the departure of any employee—should include succession planning. That means identifying a potential replacement as a backup plan of sorts for key roles. Cross-training can also help ensure that another member of the team knows a vacant role well enough to step in if needed.

What if that critical employee is the other partner? What happens if one partner becomes incapacitated? How do you handle the personal strife that pulls you away from being able to participate in the business going forward?

Consider a key man insurance policy. As partners in this business, on the advice of our financial advisor, we have taken out key man life insurance policies on each other. Such policies pay on the death of a partner, funds that can optionally be used by the surviving partner to pay the other partner's spouse for their share of the company.

Changes in the Economic or Political Landscape

These two factors present continual streams of challenges for most businesses.

The economic downturn of 2008 and 2009 impacted the country as a whole. Many businesses closed, others struggled to hang on. While most industries have managed to rebound, oil and gas—which are prominent here in Houston—have been hit very hard. That has left the oil and gas staffing part of the business struggling to gain traction.[79]

Remember, the key is to diversify your service/product offerings. For example, the oil and gas staffing side of the business experienced a downturn due to the economic downturn. However, because we were also staffing in the health care industry, we were still able to grow and thrive.

As for the political landscape, health care has been the hot topic for the last few years, and the changes in the industry have significantly affected everyone. Consumers, insurance companies and other payers, and health care providers themselves have all been dramatically affected. The same laws that have made it possible for people who didn't have insurance to receive care have left other consumers paying more for health insurance but receiving less care—simply because they can't afford better policies or because they can't afford care altogether.

And then there are the "Harveys" that end in government investigations. As we were writing this book, Facebook founder Mark Zuckerberg donned a suit and appeared before a congressional committee to explain how his vision to change the world was never intended to be used as it has been in recent years. It was never intended to be used to manipulate elections or change the way people think. Although Facebook stock has since rebounded somewhat, shareholders took quite a hit when the company was under investigation.

Even when planning involves considering any negative impacts of an idea, few entrepreneurs can foresee all the harmful ways their vision can be used. But today's economic and political arenas are highly volatile, and the only way to protect yourself from Harvey-like disasters is to be informed. Do your research and plan for the worst, and you'll be prepared as best you can be for anything that comes your way.

Remember, become involved in your industry by reading trade periodicals and joining associations. Watch for trends across industries. Keep current with any training or educational opportunities. Look for national conferences to help keep you on the cutting edge. Networking is also a powerful tool for staying prepared and heading in the right direction.

And stay up-to-date on the political landscape—that may even include monitoring bills in the legislature, lobbying to ensure that your voice is heard, contributing to political campaigns, or leveraging the power of local organizations to influence regulatory change.

For instance, we are a member of the Texas Association for Home Care & Hospice, a trade organization that acts as a unified voice in Washington, DC, for Texas-based home care and community services agencies. The organization is very proactive in positively influencing laws and regulations that affect the industry.

Similarly, changes at the local level can certainly impact business. Being active in the local community, including local politics, is even more important than being active on a state or federal level. The impact for any small business, or any individual, is at the local level. Reach out to local leaders, city offices, and representatives for your area of the state. They understand—and even drive—actions that directly affect you.

Also, as we've mentioned, join the local chamber of commerce, which is a business-driven organization. Chambers typically offer multiple networking opportunities, which can provide a variety of resources to create opportunities or serve as support if things go awry. Chamber members tend to be like-minded individuals who know what it means to be in business.

For instance, when Harvey struck, there were a number of displaced businesses that needed supplies stored in a dry place. The Fort Bend Chamber of Commerce stepped up and found someone willing to open their warehouse for storage free of charge to all members of the organization. Having those kinds of resources makes a big difference when disaster hits and you need assistance.

Being active in the community personally and professionally is also a great way of giving back. And the return on investment for volunteering time or donating funds truly seems to produce a tenfold return. The more you're out there trying to do the right thing, the better your chances when a negative occurrence threatens your reputation.

Dealing with Customer Complaints and Negative Reviews

As mentioned in principle five, "Sell Your Vision," the best way to handle negative feedback from online reviews or even customer surveys is to build up a healthy amount of positive feedback in advance. The public expects negative encounters from time to time, and positive encounters can help offset those negative ones. Again, the reality is that all the positive reviews may count for very little in the wake of a major scandal. If that happens, address it head on. Be as honest as possible—fall on the sword quickly, if you will—and earnestly own up to any mistakes or issues. Owning the story early on can help shape it in your favor and move the issue along rather than having it linger over repeated, unanswered questions, and can help diffuse the situation and lessen its long-term impact. United Airlines could have benefited from that bit of advice in 2017 when two law enforcement officers forcibly dragged a passenger off one of its planes, an incident that was videotaped and then went viral on social media. When the CEO initially responded by backing employees, company stock dropped by $1 billion. After that initial statement, repeated apologies and policy changes still couldn't repair the damage—two separate surveys later found that 40 percent of millennials said they would no longer fly the airline.[80]

Even day-to-day issues that may seem small at the time should be handled in a timely manner. While leaders tend to feel they are too busy to deal with complaints, sometimes a customer just wants to be heard. Often, all it takes is to listen and address the complaint by a senior-level person. Issues must be resolved immediately, but also by a level of personnel that satisfies the customer. We have found that the message delivered by a senior leader to an irate customer seems to be more satisfactory to them than the same message delivered by a customer service associate, someone whose role is to deal with customer problems.

That brings up a final point: Whatever the message about the company, ensure that it is consistent. If there is a scandal, control the communication from the company. Ensure all employees know that only specified personnel are to speak with media or others outside the organization. Also, take control of chat, text, and email to limit leaks that can further damage the situation.

Remember, work internally to give customers the opportunity to provide feedback rather than wait until they provide it externally— out there, it's in an environment that you can't control. And once it's there, it's out there forever.

Moving On

While start-ups do not often begin with the end goal in mind, at some point, having reached a level of success, thoughts may turn to exiting the business. When that happens, consider the purpose of the journey: Why did you start the venture in the first place? Was it to make money and then close the company and retire? Was it to grow the company and then sell it to another?

Whatever the decision, it impacts everyone associated with the business. In most situations, the exiting owner will have some nego-tiating power regarding employees—that's a real concern when an owner has built a company of people who have remained loyal over the years.

That said, there are a number of strategies for exiting a business. Here are some of the more common ones:

Merger or Acquisition

Whether the company merges with a similar business in the same industry or is bought out by a competitor, a complementing corporation, or a leading company in a completely different industry as part of a diversification strategy, the owner of the organization typically stays on in some type of management capacity for a limited time before eventually stepping away and leaving others at the helm.[81]

Take the Company Public

In some cases, an organization will issue stock to the public to essentially monetize the company. Then the exiting leader will ideally leave with a nice piece of capital and allow the organization to be run by another entity.

Sell to an Associate

At times, one partner may be ready to retire before the other. Or, an up-and-coming team member will be ready to take on the company and move it to the next level. The upside of such a transaction is that the new owner usually knows the ins and outs of the business. One of the downsides, however, may be the change in relationship between the new owner and former owner, and the new owner (formerly a coworker) as the new leader. In a situation like this, the sale can go a number of ways, including a seller financing.

Pass It to the Next Generation

In a family business, the company may be passed along to the next generation. Sometimes it remains within the founding family, sometimes it is passed to another relative.

Convert to Employee Owned

Employee stock ownership plans (ESOPs) were actually designed by Congress as vehicles for transitioning a business.[82] With an ESOP, ownership of the company transfers to employees, and the sale is made as a single transaction or in increments, for any amount of stock. The owner can stay with the company in any capacity or move on.

Turn the Company Into a Cash Cow[83]

For some individuals, retirement comes in the form of moving away from day-to-day leadership but retaining ownership of the company until a later date.

Liquidate and Close Up Shop[84]

For some owners, the goal is simply to shutter the shop and call it a day. They've worked long enough and have a nice retirement, and with the sale of the company's assets, their only plans are to take it easy.

Exiting a company built from the ground up is no easy decision. Typically, start-ups are begun by people in their thirties and forties. If, ten years later, the business is struggling to the point that the owner is considering bailing out, he or she is now another decade older. Reentering the workforce at that point can be a bit of a challenge— older, wiser, and being worth more in salary can make it harder to find opportunities for employment. That's a real concern for anyone going into business for themselves.

By the same token, exiting the working world at age fifty means a lot of years without "clocking in" somewhere. Retirement may lessen the drive for accomplishment in people who know what it means to succeed, but it rarely eliminates it altogether. What is the strategy for those days when work becomes optional? Whether it's a new venture, lending leadership talent to an area board, mentoring other businesses or individuals, or volunteering time with organizations, there are numerous options for people who have experienced success and want to share their insights and skills with others.

As we write this book, we are still evaluating our options and just beginning to consider an exit strategy. We are currently in a major growth mode, so our options may change in the years to come. Whatever the future holds, we intend to build a sustainable organization that will be around for generations.

Conclusion

Ready to Take the Leap?

With all our planning, goal setting, and organizational efforts, we still were not completely prepared for the thousand-year flood that was Hurricane Harvey. But our business model, drive for excellence, and genuine caring for others helped us pull through that disaster. Most importantly, Harvey let us see that we were on the right track. We started Sterling Staffing Solutions because we wanted to make a difference—for patients as well as for our families, our employees, our customers, and the community as a whole.

Making a difference is one reason we've shared our insights with you in this book. We hope that these principles will help you as you take on whatever you pursue in life. Now that you know what it takes—finding your niche, selling your vision, working hard, being phenomenal, doing your homework, overcoming critics, setting and understanding expectations, knowing when to delegate and when to obtain help, servant leadership, and preparing for the worst—are you willing to give it all to whatever venture you undertake?

Whatever the future holds, remember: Plan before you leap. Otherwise, you're just "leaping without a parachute." At the same time, don't over plan to the point where you never actually take the leap. The reality is that you will never have a "perfect" time to start a business. No matter how much you plan or how long you wait, you will never be experienced enough, rarely have the exact amount of capital required, never choose the perfect time to open or overall reach a level of zero uncertainty. The start of a business is a calculated risk, and if you are prepared, the risk is much better than a novice player gambling at the casino. There will always be a chance that your business may fail. However, there is also a chance that your business will succeed.

Your passion is in your "why," and that passion must drive you to *move*. You will never know whether or not you are capable of greatness unless you push yourself to the limit. Take the jump and see what you are made of. Eventually, you *must* leap.

Sterling Staffing Solutions'
S E R V I C E S

C ompanies are faced with new pressures every day, from evolving customer demands, to increasing competitive pressures, to changing legal and regulatory landscapes. Yet one thing remains certain: success in today's volatile climate hinges on a company's ability to hire the right talent, with the right skills, at the right time.

Sterling Staffing Solutions and its subsidiaries offer a comprehensive array of outsourcing and consulting services as well as top-notch staffing with a driving commitment to exceptional customer experiences:

- Sterling Medical Solutions—temporary, permanent, and project health care staffing

- Sterling Security Agents—school security consulting

- Sterling Strategic Counsel—temporary, permanent, and project legal and compliance staffing

- Sterling Education Solutions—temporary, permanent, and project education staffing

- Sterling Energy Solutions—temporary, permanent, and project oil and gas staffing

- Sterling Technology—temporary, permanent, and project technology and IT staffing

- Sterling Finance & Accounting—temporary, permanent, and project accounting and finance staffing

- Sterling Office Solutions—temporary, permanent, and project office and administrative staffing

- Sterling Construction & Infrastructure—temporary, permanent, and project construction and infrastructure staffing

Our Approach

At Sterling Staffing Solutions, we take a comprehensive approach to talent acquisition and management, aligning workforce planning and analytics with your business strategy and enabling greater workforce insight and flexibility. We call this approach "talent supply chain management"; it provides workforce solutions and consulting offerings that cover the spectrum of labor categories—from temporary and full-time hires to independent contractors to project-based workers. We offer:

- temporary/contract staffing

- direct placement

- project services

- recruitment process outsourcing

- business process outsourcing

- contingent workforce outsourcing

- career transition

- talent supply chain management

Sterling Staffing Solutions

14140 Southwest Freeway, Suite 100

Healix Building

Sugar Land, Texas 77478

Phone: 281-240-3536

www.sterlingstaffingsolutions.com

The Carter Brothers

www.thecarterbrothers.com

- The Carter Business Principles Seminars

- The Carter Business Principles Coaching

- The Carter Business Principles Speaking Series

Endnotes

1. "Hurricane Harvey Aftermath," CNN, accessed June 11, 2018, https://www.cnn.com/specials/us/hurricane-harvey.

2. Ibid.

3. "Frequently Asked Questions," SBA Office of Advocacy," September 2012, accessed April 2, 2018, https://www.sba.gov/sites/default/files/FAQ_Sept_2012.pdf.

4. "Facts & Data on Small Business and Entrepreneurship," Small Business & Entrepreneurship Council, accessed April 2, 2018, http://sbecouncil.org/about-us/facts-and-data.

5. Simon Sinek Inc., accessed April 2, 2018, https://startwithwhy.com/find-your-why.

6. Charles River Editors, *The Top 5 Greatest Artists: Leonardo, Michelangelo, Raphael, Vincent Van Gogh, and Pablo Picasso*, CreateSpace Independent Publishing Platform: September 10, 2013.

7. *Merriam-Webster*, *s.v.* "partnership," https://www.merriam-webster.com/dictionary/partnership.

8 "Marriage & Divorce," American Psychological Association, accessed April 1, 2018, http://www.apa.org/topics/divorce.

9 Amanda Neville, "Why Partnership Is Harder Than Marriage," *Forbes*, May 1, 2013, accessed April 1, 2018, https://www.forbes.com/sites/amandaneville/2013/03/01/why-partnership-is-harder-than-marriage/#312564287ec9; Susan Ward, "Why Business Partnerships Fail," The Balance, March 15, 2018, accessed April 1, 2018, https://www.thebalance.com/why-business-partnerships-fail-4107045.

10 Ibid.

11 Malini Bhatia, "3 Things Happy Marriages and Successful Business Partnerships Have in Common," Inc.com, February 1, 2018, accessed April 1, 2018, https://www.inc.com/young-entrepreneur-council/3-things-happy-marriages-successful-business-partnerships-have-in-common.html?cid=search.

12 C. Curley, "The Risks and Benefits of Equity Partnerships," National Federation of Independent Business, October 26, 2011, accessed April 1, 2018, https://www.nfib.com/content/resources/money/the-risks-and-benefits-of-equity-partnerships-58519.

13 The Myers & Briggs Foundation, http://www.myersbriggs.org/.

14 "DiSC Overview," DiSCProfile, https://www.discprofile.com/.

15 "History of Berkshire Hathaway," WarrenBuffett.com, accessed June 8, 2018, https://www.warrenbuffett.com/berkshire-hathaway/history-of-berkshire-hathaway.

16 "Taco Bell History," Taco Bell, accessed June 8, 2018, https://www.tacobell.com/history.

17 Justin Kautz, "Taco Bell," Encyclopaedia Brittanica, accessed June 8, 2018, https://www.britannica.com/topic/Taco-Bell.

18 "Experience Avon's History," Avon, accessed June 8, 2018, http://www.avoncompany.com/aboutavon/history/index.html.

19 "Section 1: 10-Q (FORM 10-Q)," Avon Products Inc. quarterly filing, March 31, 2018, accessed June 8, 2018, http://investor.avoncompany.com/AsReportedViewer. aspx?id=393320093#SNL_131.

20 "About Tiffany & Co.," Tiffany & Co. for the Press, accessed June 8, 2018, http://press.tiffany.com/ViewBackgrounder. aspx?backgrounderId=33.

21 "Shareholder Information," Tiffany & Co., accessed June 8, 2018, http://investor.tiffany.com/news-releases/news-release-details/ tiffany-reports-fiscal-2017-results.

22 Scott Leibs, "Grow. Hire. Repeat," *Inc.,* February 25, 2014, accessed April 24, 2018, https://www.inc.com/ magazine/201403/scott-leibs/sustained-growth-predicts-business-success.html.

23 Ibid.

24 Ibid.

25 Neil Petch, "The Five Stages of Your Business Lifecycle: Which Phase Are You In?" *Entrepreneur,* February 29, 2016, accessed March 18, 2018, https://www.entrepreneur.com/ article/271290.

26 Scott Leibs, "Grow. Hire. Repeat," *Inc.,* February 25, 2014, accessed April 24, 2018, https://www.inc.com/ magazine/201403/scott-leibs/sustained-growth-predicts-business-success.html.

27 Jill Aitoro, "Should Northrop Grumman Have Held On to Shipbuilding?" *Washington Business Journal,* March 18, 2014, accessed April 18, 2018, https://www.bizjournals.com/washington/blog/fedbiz_daily/2014/03/should-northrop-grumman-have-held-on-to.html.

28 Dean Takahashi, "How Zynga Grew from Gaming Outcast to $9 Billion Social Game Powerhouse," *Venture Beat,* December 12, 2011, accessed April 22, 2018, https://venturebeat.com/2011/12/12/zynga-history/view-all.

29 David Aaker, "Why Wasn't the iPod a Sony Brand? Prophet, March 5, 2011, accessed April 18, 2018, https://www.prophet.com/2011/03/12-why-wasnt-the-ipod-a-sony-brand.

30 Michael Pascoe, "What to Learn from Sony's Greatest Mistake," *Sydney Morning Herald*, June 28, 2012, accessed April 18, 2018, https://www.smh.com.au/business/what-to-learn-from-sonys-greatest-mistake-20120628-21405.html.

31 Glenn Solomon, "Transitioning from a Startup to Growth-Stage Company," *Fortune*, February 11, 2013, accessed March 18, 2018, http://fortune.com/2013/02/11/transitioning-from-a-startup-to-growth-stage-company.

32 "Employee Development: How to Grow Your Employees When You Can't Promote Them," Lighthouse, accessed July 11, 2018, https://getlighthouse.com/blog/employee-development-grow-cant-promote/.

33 Ibid.

34 "Global Trust in Advertising: Winning Strategies for an Evolving Media Landscape," The Nielsen Company, September 2015, accessed April 19, 2018, https://www.nielsen.com/content/dam/nielsenglobal/apac/docs/reports/2015/nielsen-global-trust-in-advertising-report-september-2015.pdf.

35 Ibid.

36 Mindi Chahal, "Social Commerce: How Willing Are Consumers to Buy Through Social Media?" *Marketing Week,* March 23, 2016, accessed April 19, 2018, https://www.marketingweek.com/2016/03/23/social-commerce-how-willing-are-consumers-to-buy-through-social-media.

37 Alex York, "61 Social Media Statistics to Bookmark for 2018," SproutSocial, February 19, 2018, accessed April 19, 2018, https://sproutsocial.com/insights/social-media-statistics.

38 Ibid.

39 Ibid.

40 Nem Radenovic, "The Importance of Timeliness in Digital Marketing," Digital Brand Lounge, April 1, 2017, accessed April 19, 2018, https://nrdigitalbranding.com/blog/ importance-of-timeliness-in-digital-marketing.

41 Quoted in Tim Devaney and Tom Stein, "Handling Haters: How to Respond to Negative Online Reviews," *Forbes*, March 3, 2014, accessed April 19, 2018, https://www.forbes.com/ sites/sage/2014/03/03/handling-haters-how-to-respond-to-negative-online-reviews/#47191cc56a85.

42 Áine Cain, "11 Insanely Cool Benefits for Facebook Employees," *Inc.*, November 9, 2017, accessed June 9, 2018, https://www. inc.com/business-insider/facebook-employee-perks-benefits-united-states-california-mark-zuckerberg.html.

43 Jillian D'Onfro and Lucy England, "An Inside Look at Google's Best Employee Perks," *Inc.*, September 21, 2015, accessed June 9, 2018, https://www.inc.com/business-insider/best-google-benefits.html.

44 Chris Hurn, "Stuffed Giraffe Shows What Customer Service Is All About," *Huffington Post*, blog post, May 17, 2012, accessed June 9, 2018, https://www.huffingtonpost.com/chris-hurn/ stuffed-giraffe-shows-wha_b_1524038.html.

45 Kim Cameron et. al., "Effects of Positive Practices on Organizational Effectiveness," *Journal of Applied Behavioral Science* 47, no. 3 (Jan. 26, 2011), http://journals.sagepub.com/doi/ pdf/10.1177/0021886310395514.

46 Emma Seppala, "Positive Teams Are More Productive," *Harvard Business Review,* March 18, 2015, accessed June 9, 2018, https://hbr.org/2015/03/positive-teams-are-more-productive.

47 Sujan Patel, "10 Examples of Companies with Fantastic Cultures," *Entrepreneur,* August 6, 2015, accessed June 9, 2018, https://www.entrepreneur.com/article/249174.

48 Charles Trevail et. al., "The Brands That Make Customers Feel Respected," *Harvard Business Review,* November 01, 2016, accessed June 9, 2018, https://hbr.org/2016/11/the-brands-that-make-customers-feel-respected.

49 Glen White, "Continuous Innovation at Boeing Leads to Success in a Highly Competitive Industry," Global Manufacturing, October 23, 2014, https://www.manufacturingglobal.com/lean-manufacturing/continuous-innovation-boeing-leads-success-highly-competitive-industry.

50 Jennifer Calfas, "This Furniture Store Has Converted into a Makeshift Shelter for Harvey Victims," *Time,* August 28, 2017, accessed June 9, 2018, http://time.com/4919017/gallery-furniture-houston-harvey-hurricane-shelter.

51 "Careers & Jobs: Become an Officer in the U.S. Army," accessed April 23, 2018, https://www.goarmy.com/careers-and-jobs/become-an-officer.html.

52 "Careers & Jobs: Becoming an Army Officer," U.S. Army, accessed April 21, 2018, https://www.goarmy.com/careers-and-jobs/become-an-officer/how-to-become-an-officer-in-the-army.html.

53 "Who Were They?" Tuskegee Airmen National Historical Museum website, accessed April 23, 2018, http://www.tuskegeemuseum.org/who-were-they.

54 Excerpt from "How the GOAT Was Built: Six Life Lessons from the 1996 Chicago Bulls" by Jack M. Silverstein, as quoted in: Readjack, "'My Coach Is Everything'"—Phil Jackson's influence on the 1996 Chicago Bulls," ReadJack.com, May 22, 2016, accessed April 22, 2018, https://readjack.wordpress.com/2016/05/22/phil-jackson-influence-1996-chicago-bulls.

55 Roland Lazenby, *Michael Jordan: The Life* (New York: Little, Brown, 2014).

56 Kelli Richards, "The Secret Weapon of Billionaire CEOs and Other Wildly Successful People," *Inc.,* October 10, 2014, accessed April 21, 2018, https://www.inc.com/kelli-richards/the-secret-weapon-of-billionaire-ceos-and-other-wildly-successful-people.html.

57 Richard Trenchard, "Five Business Leaders Who Have a Mentor to Thank for Their Success," Virgin, July 8, 2016, accessed June 9, 2018, https://www.virgin.com/entrepreneur/five-business-leaders-who-have-mentor-thank-their-success.

58 Ibid.

59 Ibid.

60 "Garrett Morgan," Biography, accessed June 10, 2018, https://www.biography.com/people/garrett-morgan-9414691.

61 Stephanie Vozza, "Why Employees at Apple And Google Are More Productive," Fast Company, March 13, 2017, https://www.fastcompany.com/3068771/how-employees-at-apple-and-google-are-more-productive.

62 "Study Suggests Medical Errors Now Third Leading Cause of Death in the U.S.," news release, Johns Hopkins Medicine, May 3, 2016, accessed May 4, 2018, https://www.hopkinsmedicine.org/news/media/releases/study_suggests_medical_errors_now_third_leading_cause_of_death_in_the_us; Ray Sipherd, "The Third-Leading Cause of Death in US Most Doctors Don't Want You to Know About," CNBC, February 22, 2018, https://www.cnbc.com/2018/02/22/medical-errors-third-leading-cause-of-death-in-america.html.

63 "Volvo Cars Named as One of the World's Most Ethical Companies in 2018," news release, Volvo Car Group, February 12, 2018, accessed June 10, 2018, https://www.media.volvocars.com/global/en-gb/media/pressreleases/223159/volvo-cars-named-as-one-of-the-worlds-most-ethical-companies-in-2018.

64 "Dell Inc. Named One of World's Most Ethical Companies for 2018," news release, Dell, February 12, 2018, accessed June 10, 2018, http://www.dell.com/learn/us/en/uscorp1/press-releases/2018-02-12-dell-inc-named-one-of-worlds-most-ethical-companies-for-2018.

65 "Standards of Business Conduct," Microsoft, accessed June 10, 2018, https://www.microsoft.com/en-us/legal/compliance/sbc/default.aspx.

66 "For Second Consecutive Year, Grupo Bimbo Is Included In the List of the World's Most Ethical Companies, Made by the Ethisphere Institute," news release, Grupo Bimbo, February 13, 2018, accessed June 10, 2018, https://www.grupobimbo.com/en/press-room/release/second-consecutive-year-grupo-bimbo-included-list-worlds-most-ethical-companies.

67 Firas Kittaneh, "Open Letter to Aspiring Entrepreneurs: Don't Reinvent the Wheel," *Inc.*, January 8, 2018, https://www.inc.com/firas-kittaneh/open-letter-to-aspiring-entrepreneurs-dont-reinvent-wheel.html.

68 Andrew Zaleski, "Seven Businesses that Cloned Others and Made Millions," CNBC online, October 4, 2017, https://www.cnbc.com/2017/10/03/7-businesses-that-cloned-others-and-made-millions.html; Sam Weber, "The Ground War Between FedEx and UPS," PBS, August 25, 2010, http://www.pbs.org/wnet/need-to-know/economy/the-ground-war-between-fedex-and-ups/3095/.

69 Christiaan Hetzner and Luca Ciferri, "Mercedes, BMW and Audi Extend Reach at the Expense of Mass-Market Brands," Automotive News, September 14, 2015, accessed May 4, 2018, http://www.autonews.com/article/20150914/RETAIL/309149948/mercedes-bmw-and-audi-extend-reach-at-the-expense-of-mass-market.

70 Sam Levin, "'We're Watching a Company Explode': Is Snapchat Becoming Irrelevant?" Guardian, February 28, 2018, accessed May 4, 2018, https://www.theguardian.com/technology/2018/feb/23/snapchat-redesign-scandal-kylie-jenner-what-went-wrong.

71 Ibid.

72 Emma Stefansky, "Snapchat Lost $800 Million after Rihanna Criticized Its Offensive Ad," Vanity Fair, March 17, 2018, May 4, 2018, https://www.vanityfair.com/style/2018/03/rihanna-chris-brown-snapchat-ad.

73 Levin, Sam, "'We're Watching a Company Explode': Is Snapchat Becoming Irrelevant?" Guardian, February 28, 2018, accessed May 4, 2018, https://www.theguardian.com/technology/2018/feb/23/snapchat-redesign-scandal-kylie-jenner-what-went-wrong.

74 Chris Mooney, "Hurricane Harvey Was Year's Costliest U.S. Disaster at $125 Billion in Damages," Texas Tribune, January 8, 2018, accessed June 11, 2018, https://www.texastribune.org/2018/01/08/hurricane-harvey-was-years-costliest-us-disaster-125-billion-damages.

75 Ernest Scheyder, "For Houston Homeowners, Tough Decisions on Whether to Rebuild," Reuters, September 5, 2017, accessed June 11, 2018, https://www.reuters.com/article/us-storm-harvey-housing/for-houston-homeowners-tough-decisions-on-whether-to-rebuild-idUSKCN1BG0HD.

76 Lance Ulanoff, "Tim Cook as Apple CEO: Still Winning," Mashable, August 24, 2016, accessed June 10, 2018, https://mashable.com/2016/08/24/time-cook-apple-ceo-5-year-anniversary/#7xzV7BeIOaqW.

77 Lucinda Shen, "Apple Is Worth Over $900 Billion. but It Won't Be the World's First Trillion-Dollar Company," *Fortune*, November 8, 2017, accessed June 10, 2018, http://fortune.com/2017/11/08/apple-stock-amazon-trillion-aapl-iphone-x/.

78 Aaron Smith, "Steve Jobs' Departure Pushes Apple Stock Down 2.25%," CNN Money, January 18, 2011, accessed June 10, 2018, http://money.cnn.com/2011/01/18/technology/apple_jobs/index.htm.

79 Jude Clemente, "The Link Between Crude Oil and Gasoline Prices," *Forbes*, June 27, 2018, https://www.forbes.com/sites/judeclemente/2018/06/27/the-link-between-crude-oil-and-gasoline-prices/#2166abfb37db.

80 Sean Czarnecki, "Timeline of a Crisis: United Airlines," *PR Week,* June 06, 2017, accessed June 10, 2018, https://www.prweek.com/article/1435619/timeline-crisis-united-airlines.

81 Martin Zwilling, "Five Smart Exit Strategies," *Business Insider*, January 5, 2011, accessed May 8, 2018, http://www.businessinsider.com/startup-exits-should-be-positive-and-planned-early-2011-1.

82 "Using an Employee Stock Ownership Plan (ESOP) for Business Continuity in a Closely Held Company," National Center for Employee Ownership, accessed May 8, 2018, https://www.nceo.org/articles/esop-business-continuity.

83 Martin Zwilling, "Five Smart Exit Strategies," *Business Insider,* January 5, 2011, accessed May 8, 2018, http://www.businessinsider.com/startup-exits-should-be-positive-and-planned-early-2011-1.

84 Ibid.